THE
WITCH'S COMPANION

SORAYA

With contributions by Kit Berry, Robin Darkmere,
and Anna Franklin

Soraya would like to thank all the contributors for
their invaluable additions to this book
Blessed be!

Published 2017 by Waverley Books,
an imprint of The Gresham Publishing Company Ltd, Academy Park,
Building 4000, Gower Street, Glasgow, G51 1PR, Scotland
www.waverley-books.co.uk
info@waverley-books.co.uk
Find us on facebook/pages/waverleybooks

First published 2011. Reprinted 2015, 2016, 2017.

Contents

Meditation   **159**

Introduction

Over the past few years since I finished my *Book of Spells* I have received hundreds of emails from readers telling me how much they enjoyed my book. But many emails came from readers asking me the same question 'where do I start?' In this book I will try to answer that question and provide information on all manner of resources that can be used both for the new and the experienced witch.

I can remember when I first began to follow my path, if I was trying to find a piece of information, more often than not I would have to look at three or four different books. The purpose of this book is to try to provide you with one single book containing as much helpful information as I can find to help you to find what you are looking for with relative ease.

It appears that a large number of people believe that being a Pagan is all about creating magick, and casting spells. It's not. Of course being able to change things by the power of one's will is a desirable side effect but that is not what being a Pagan is about. Following a Wiccan or Pagan path is about knowing yourself inside and out. Following this path is about knowing right from wrong in every aspect of your life. Being a Pagan means having respect for every living thing, appreciating the beauty and fragility of Mother Earth and everything on around and related to it.

The earth, wind and sea; the seasons, the sun, the moon and the stars; they are all important to a Pagan. We don't take anything that doesn't belong to us. If we do then someone will take from us three times over. We don't harm anyone or someone will harm us three times over.

As a member of the Pagan Federation I live by these three principles:

i.   Love for and Kinship with Nature. Reverence for the life force and its ever-renewing cycles of life and death
ii. A Positive Morality in which the individual is responsible for the discovery and development of their true nature in harmony with the outer world and community. This is often expressed as 'Do what you will, as long as it harms none'.
iii. Recognition of the Divine, which transcends gender, acknowledging both the female and male aspect of the Deity.

What's in a Name?

Magic and Magick

Some Pagans consider those who use the spelling of magick with a 'k' at the end not to be serious pagans. They suggest it implies they might be self-taught from less-than-serious books. I'd say to that, aren't we all self-taught in a way? We may attend classes or courses or groups to learn about any subject but it's only practice (that is more often than not done alone) that gives us the full knowledge and experience of something.

And for me, and many others, 'magic' is the word for something that is done by conjurers who earn money from enthralling audiences with trickery and sleight of hand. I use the word 'magick' to differentiate the art of causing change – which is what Witches, Wiccans or Pagans do – from mere theatrical trickery. You can get too hung up on these kind of debates about what is really just a spelling difference. In the end, what most matters is that your intention is good.

However, if you need a reason to use the word magick, the vibration of the numbers corresponding to the letters of the words magic and magick is quite significant. As a numerologist I look at all these influences.

The word 'magic' creates a vibration which could mean indecision or confusion whereas applying the k at the end to create 'magick' creates a vibration which means stimulation, creation and fertility.

The letters of the alphabet correspond to the numbers one to nine. Each number has a special significance. I'm afraid there isn't space to go into the subject of numerology in-depth here. For that, best to consult specialist books on the subject. Numerology is also mentioned briefly on page 111-112, and page 173 in this book, and in my *Book of Spells*.

Wiccan, Witch or Pagan

A great debate exists between some people in the Pagan community about the use of the words Wiccan, Witch, and Pagan. My personal observation is that when people who are unfamiliar with modern neopaganism hear the word 'Pagan' they are put off, thinking of the definition 'heathen' and that the person who is Pagan doesn't believe in God, or worse, is some sort of devil worshipper. I don't really need to add that this is not the case.

On the other hand, when the same person hears the word 'Wiccan' the reaction is more likely to be 'Oh, what's that?' and this gives one the opportunity to give a proper explanation of one's beliefs.

In the strictest terms, Wicca is a belief system that worships a Goddess and a God – Lady and Lord. The Goddess, the feminine side of divinity, is a Triple Goddess (the Maiden, the Mother and the Crone). The God is known as The Horned God and is the masculine side of divinity.

Wicca always existed but it was popularised in the early 20th century by Gerald Gardner (see page 23). Gerald Gardner based his teachings on ancient witchcraft traditions, the teachings of the New Forest Coven and on his own research into pre-Christian Pagan worship. Some people believe that only traditions with a lineage back to Gerald Gardner can be called Wiccan but increasingly the word is becoming synonymous with witchcraft.

The practice of Wicca most probably dates back at least 25,000 years but the use of the term in our modern society to describe those who practise witchcraft is relatively new.

The original meaning of the word 'Pagan' was simply someone who lived in the country. Bear in mind that way back in time, when there was only the horse for transport (if you were lucky), just surviving the elements and finding food was a full-time job. Nowadays when we are ill we can lift the phone and have a visit from a doctor. To survive in those days you had to have certain skills or at least know someone who had and then you could barter for what you needed. If you were sick you went to the 'wise woman', an old woman who would prepare a herbal draft which might cure you. That must have seemed like magick. In real terms, the old woman (the crone) was just someone who had learned about natural remedies and the healing properties of plants. She was the original Wiccan – a wise one.

Wicca

If you need some more explanations about Wicca, the following are the beliefs that most Wiccans hold.

As mentioned, Wiccans believe in and Worship the Lord and Lady, the God and Goddess. There are many names for the God and Goddess in different traditions, or in different countries – but they are still the God and Goddess.

Wiccans follow what has become known as the Wiccan Rede: 'An it harm none, do what ye will', 'if it harms no one, do as you like' (page 42).

Wiccans believe in reincarnation. They believe that fertility, the cycle of life and rebirth are all interconnected. Fertility is an important part of

Wicca – the union of God and Goddess. When you think of the Goddess you should be thinking Mother Earth. The God is represented by the Sun. In the cycle of the seasons the Sun (the God) warms the Earth (the Goddess). In this heat she becomes fertile and begins to produce young (seeds) as the season moves the earth turns, the weather becomes colder, the Sun begins his seasonal death. The Goddess becomes cold but before she does we harvest her bounty. She sinks deeper into the earth and rests until it's time to return but we are reminded of her presence by the returning cycles of the moon. This whole cycle is repeated in our lives. We are born, develop, mature, couple, produce our seed, give birth, grow old and return to the earth until its time to reincarnate and it all begins again.

This representation of fertility is symbolically represented by placing the point of the athame or wand or even a finger into wine or water during a ceremony. Couples, married or otherwise committed, who work together may actually perform this union because magick requires raising considerable loving pure energy and there is no more powerful energy than that raised between loving couples. This is called The Great Rite. Not everyone is in a relationship that allows this but the relationship between coven friends is loving, so energy can be raised by dance or by voice chanting or singing or by other methods such as spiralling or visualisation and then symbolically represented. In the unlikely event that you encounter a coven promoting sex, steer clear!

One final point – in numerology the words Wicca and Pagan have the same numerical vibration, which corresponds to fertility so, really, it makes no difference what you call yourself! It's how you behave that makes the difference.

White Witch

For those who wish to follow a path that uses magick there is only one path to follow and that is of magick performed wholly for the good. This has become known in the popular media as white magick. Some say that magick can be black or evil, white or good, but the truth is there is no black, evil, good or white magick – it's all the same. There are, however, good people and evil people. 'White witch' has come to be the term used to describe someone who would never use their skills powers or knowledge to harm anyone, always thinks of the repercussions their actions, and might use their powers for healing.

What Discipline?

What kind of Pagan are you? What discipline will you follow? There are many different practices. Some people work within a coven and others work alone as Solitaries. Think about what your aims are from becoming a witch. What areas of Paganism are you drawn to? You shouldn't approach it lightly. You don't need to join a group to find your path – at least not at first. Do as much reading as you can, and not just about witchcraft. Think about nature and the environment and any subjects that you are particularly interested in or feel passionate about. These will all help you on your way.

Covens

A coven is made up of a group of people who meet on a regular basis to celebrate Pagan festivals or for the purpose of simply getting together to learn and share. The coven would comprise men and women who would be known as priests and priestesses and they would be led by a High Priest and a High Priestess.

Some people begin to follow the Wiccan or Pagan path as a Solitary and continue to practice as a Solitary, whilst others look for a coven to join. The advantage of working as a Solitary is that you can work and develop at your own pace. The disadvantage is that being a Solitary can be quite an isolating occupation. Today though we are blessed with the Internet giving us the opportunity to network and speak to like-minded people even though we still carry out our rituals alone.

Joining a coven is making a commitment to more than the craft, it is making a commitment to the High Priestess and High Priest of the coven as well as the other members. Each coven will have its own methods practices and teachings and you will be expected to adhere to these practices and develop through various degrees of initiation.

How do you look for a coven? Some covens have outer circles that you can join. If you have any new age shops nearby you could ask advice about local groups in there. There are also gatherings called 'moots' where you can go to meet fellow pagans. Join an online forum like the Pagan Network or like my Witches Web where others can maybe advise you about local events.

Be aware of your personal safety. You will usually have to make a formal request to join a coven. Covens don't usually seek out new members so be wary of any that do. And never pay money to do so! Don't ignore your gut instinct about these things.

Some covens insist newcomers study the Craft for (at least) a year and a day before Initiation and then a year and day between degrees or levels. Everyone is different though – some need more time than others before they are ready.

No reputable coven will accept anyone under the age of 18, or want to you to break the law. No-one in the coven should have more power than all the rest, even if they are High Priest or Priestess. Some covens perform their rituals 'sky clad' (nude with a robe), you need to decide if you are comfortable with that. And if anyone insists that sex must be part of your initiation avoid them like the plague!

Solitaries

A Solitary witch doesn't belong to a coven. They are often self-initiated.

Self-initiation is a declaration of your promise to your God or Goddess, to live in harmony with nature to the best of your abilities. There are many proclaimed Witches, Wiccans or Pagans who have never been initiated by a High Priestess nor performed a Self-initiation Ceremony and yet they are no less witches, Wiccans or Pagans. They are what they are by their words, deeds and actions. However, a Self-initiation Ceremony is a beautiful, fulfilling ritual to perform.

Those who feel that Wiccans must train in a coven and be properly initiated are by their views showing the Wiccan belief that we should have respect for others and the way in which they honour their God or Goddess.

It is also easier, but no less reverent, to learn from the experiences of others and to be helped in the right direction by a mentor than to have to work it all out for yourself from the pages of books.

One way or another, the decision to work alone or in a coven, or when to join a coven if you have been a Solitary, is your decision alone and destiny will guide your choice and set the timing in place.

If you have not yet performed a Self-initiation Ceremony, or as it is sometimes called a Self-dedication Ceremony, and you would like to do so, the best time of year is Imbolc (February 2nd, which is sometimes known as Candlemas or Oimelc). At this time, the Goddess (Mother Earth) is beginning to awaken from her deep winter seclusion and rest. As She reveals herself we see evidence of this in the early appearance of snowdrops or crocus.

As the time passes you can observe each Sabbat and Esbat and observe the changes in the seasons and how Mother Earth reacts to these changes. You will grow from strength to strength in your knowledge understanding and confidence. You will find a Self-dedication Ceremony in this book (see page 58) and you can follow it to the letter or use it for guidance as you create your own ceremony.

Although I was initiated by the High Priestess of a coven, I have mostly practised my craft as a Solitary. Sometimes I've worked with others in the physical sense. I also have several online sisters and brothers who have joined the Witches Web, my online forum, and we keep in touch with each other by email and occasional phone calls. I suppose you could call that my cyber coven.

I have from time to time performed initiations with novices of the craft who have requested this blessing from me and I have been honoured by their request.

In the past I have lived in fairly remote locations preventing me from being part of a working coven, however, since my move to Argyll things have changed. It appears that the Goddess has decided that I should have my own coven and I now have the joy of working with some lovely friends of a like mind. We learn from each other and share sabbats and esbats. Having found them I wonder how I managed without them. They are my friends, my students and my karmic sisters.

Kitchen Witches

Kitchen Witches are usually supportive of green issues and will also produce their own self-grown herbal remedies and potions. A lot of Solitaries are Green Witches or Kitchen Witches but they may, from time to time, join other groups for celebrations.

As with all faiths there are offshoots and varieties and that is because everyone is different and their needs are different too. Wicca or Paganism is something that you believe in and practise in a way that suits you.

Green Witch or Hedge Witch

A Green or Hedge Witch more often than not works alone, cares for their environment and generally has a keen interest in natural remedies, particularly those which have been handed down through the years. Hedge Witches often clean rubbish that other people leave lying on roadsides picnic areas and beaches. Two of my Hedge Witch friends do this on a regular basis. That's not to say that they are they only ones who do this. Nor is everyone who voluntarily cleans up roadside garbage a witch.

Green Witches focus on the earth and are likely to be involved in replenishing or restocking wasteland to introduce trees, shrubs, flora and fauna that may be dying because of pollution or mankind's general neglect or abuse

I am proud to say that I have come to know, and consider as a friend, **Kit Berry** a Green or Natural Witch, writer of *The Magus of Stonewylde*, *Moondance of Stonewylde*, and *Solstice of Stonewylde*. Her contribution below shouts in a loud voice all that I believe about being a Pagan. This current book hopefully provides everything that you, the reader will require should you wish to perform casual, ritualistic, or full-blown ceremonies but remember you need nothing more than a pure heart and a clear intention to honour the Lord and Lady and to say thanks or ask for a blessing.

I am sure that you will enjoy reading Kit's contribution of what I would call natural magick.

From Kit Berry, author of the Stonewylde Series of books:

To me, organised worship and spirituality are generally mutually exclusive. I do enjoy and appreciate the power of ritual and ceremony, the beauty of repetition and custom. As a youngster I sang in the church choir and loved the well-known order of service, the hymns and bells, incense and psalms. It was all comforting and familiar. But it did nothing for me spiritually. I couldn't believe in all the things I sang and prayed about. They were just beautiful but empty words and gestures. I came to Paganism quite late in life, although like many, when I eventually did it felt like a home-coming, a return to the place where I truly belonged.

I was led here by a hare, one sunny summer's afternoon in the woods. She sat on the path before me, blocking my way, and looked me deep in the eye. It was a magical encounter and changed my life. I didn't know then that the hare is a creature of transformation, a shape-shifter who can not only change herself but also transform others. She certainly transformed me and gave my life a new direction and purpose.

However, even as a free and wild Pagan, I found that organised ritual and ceremony were just not for me. It was wonderful to find that here was a spirituality where that didn't matter, where I didn't have to follow rules and dogma. 'An it harm none, do what you will' was music to my ears.

I understand that many Pagans enjoy organised ceremonies and performing set rituals, and feel there's a power in doing things this way. But for me, as soon as words are written or recited and procedures adhered to, I just lose all sense of awe and spontaneity. I need to be free and able to find my own silver thread to the source, and this thread changes all the time.

I celebrate the eight festivals in varying ways. Sometimes I observe sunrise and sunset, sometimes I visit a special or sacred place and sometimes I perform my own private and perhaps elaborate ritual. I may use candles and symbols if that feels appropriate. At other times I just meditate, out of doors if possible. Sometimes I like to gather objects for their beauty and to help me focus, maybe arranged on an altar or maybe just on the ground in a nest of grass. As Paganism is to me a religion of nature, I prefer these objects to be natural. Conkers and acorns in the autumn, sunflowers in the summer, ears of wheat, corn and barley at harvest time, for example. Whatever I can find and whatever feels right - there are absolutely no hard and fast rules.

The same goes for the moon. At the full moon I have, in the past, cast a circle, called the elements, raised the energy. I've used fire and water, salt and symbols, been both sky clad and elaborately robed. The very first time I cast a circle formally was during a lunar eclipse at the Wolf Moon in January, several years ago. It was a very powerful and moving experience indeed. Afterwards when I tried to turn the light on, I fused the whole house and the flash from the light-switch made a scorch mark right up the wall! Lately I simply stand outside in my garden and gaze at the full moon, drawing on her beauty and energy and focussing my intent. This feels right for now, but doubtless that will change at some point.

I think that many folk share my aversion to formalised ritual and prefer simple spontaneity. My very favourite act of spirituality, and when I feel most in tune with the Goddess and the Green Man, is when I'm out walking alone. I love being up high amongst hills, or on cliff-tops near the sea, or deep within woods. I feel an uplifting of my soul and a strange sense of aligning myself with the incredible power and energy all around. This is my best act of 'worship'.

Each to their own – should anyone need a label, I call this 'Green Magic' and think of myself as a green witch. I know there are plenty of others who feel this sense of connection through the simple act of being alone and surrounded by the glory of nature. I also know from the many people who write to me having read my books without any previous knowledge of Paganism, that the prospect of learning masses of words and rituals is daunting. After reading *Stonewylde*, many feel a deep and almost instant affinity and want to call themselves Pagans, but worry about using the wrong colour candle for a ceremony or the wrong type of herbs.

There is of course a body of lore and knowledge, a wisdom that can be learned and used, and which is a very important part of the Craft. But there's also the danger of focussing too much on this and forgetting what your heart tells you. So I would say to anyone new to Paganism – honour the Goddess and the Green Man in whatever way feels right for you. Recognise that like the moon, your needs and spirituality will change constantly, waxing and waning, sometimes being obscured by clouds and sometimes blazing in full glory.

To me, there are no right and wrong ways other than those wise words – 'An it harm none, do what you will.'

Herbal Witchcraft

Some time ago I received an email from **Robin Darkmere** and we began to correspond on a regular basis. I would say that we have become good friends although we have still to meet – we have exchanged Christmas gifts, emails, fallen about laughing at each other while we attempted to have a sensible conversation and view each other's webcams. I hope you enjoy reading Robin's contribution as much as I did.

From Robin Darkmere, Magister de Glastonbury:

Modern Western herbal medicine has its roots firmly based in witchcraft and with this in mind; it conjures up images of an old woman stirring a cauldron of boiling liquid with a black cat at her side. Shakespeare has a lot to answer for when the word witch is mentioned. But no matter what images are brought to mind, there is no denying that herbalism and witchcraft go hand in hand.

The tools of the craft are very often cleansed using the smoke from smouldering sage leaves before their ritual usage. Herbs such as rosemary are used in spells that are remembering or honouring the dead, in fact, I cannot imagine performing my spellcraft without herbs being present on my altar.

But herbs are not just for cleansing purposes or for divination. They can also be used in simple medicines, as well as culinary witchcraft. Witchcraft isn't just confined to the conjuring room or the altar or whatever sacred space has been put aside to perform such rituals and spells. Witchcraft can be used all over the home and especially in the kitchen.

The Goddess is all powerful and all creative. Everything that we are and everything we see around us is of her. So, when we cook a meal for ourselves and our families, there is no reason as to why witchcraft cannot be performed over the food we are preparing, cooking, and ultimately eating. The same goes for preparing medicines in the kitchen using herbs. A cough syrup made from marigolds is very effective in fighting a tickly cough, but a marigold cough syrup that has had the Goddess's powers invoked into it, will be much more powerful.

So how are the Goddess's powers invoked into a simple herbal medicine? It's not as difficult as it sounds. The easiest way is to gather together everything you are going to use and place it all on the worktop before you. Spend a little time with your eyes closed and breathing deeply. Focus your mind on the Goddess, the medicine you are going to make and the effect you want it to have on the ailment you are treating. Next open the protective circle and call upon the elements of Earth, Air, Fire and Water to guard you, guide you, and protect you, during the spell. Hold up each ingredient and ask the Goddess's blessing upon each one.

As you follow the recipe and stir whatever it is you are making, ask the Goddess to bless the potion and to send her healing powers into it. Once made and bottled, the Goddess's blessing again can be asked for on the finished product before it is used.

Invoking the powers of the deities on cooking ingredients and medicines etc. is not a new thing; in fact the earliest humans to walk the earth were thought to have asked the blessing of the Gods before going out hunting and killing an animal for food. In the same kind of light, using herbs to heal wounds and cure illnesses isn't new either.

A few years ago an archaeological dig in Iraq came across a Neolithic grave. Amongst the bones of the dead person that was buried were found mummified leaves of various plants. When these remains were taken to the laboratory for analysis, they were found to be plants that are known today for their healing properties.

The Greeks and the Romans were also well acquainted with herbs for healing and they too invoked the powers of their Gods to give the medicines a supernatural boost. Herbs were used in the Temples of the Egyptians and the Babylonians, cultures all over the globe have used herbs in rituals and medicines with the invocation of their Gods.

Once the art of modern medicine got a grip on British society back in the seventeenth century, it became a whole new world of science and technology. Anatomy and physiology could be studied at university and degrees were handed out. Doctors began to practise medicine and it wasn't cheap. Modern medicine was out of the reach of most of the working populace.

They turned to the wise woman who lived on the outskirts of the village or down the lane in the wood or forest. The wise woman was never a real part of the community; she kept herself to herself and never went to church with the rest of the village. Surrounded by myth and legends, these wise women and cunning men were thought to have the gift of divination and were able to cure the ills of anyone who approached them for their help.

The wise woman was the local midwife and would be present at the birth of most of the villagers' children. Inside her cottage would be jars of herbs and potions and a cauldron would be bubbling on the fire. So it is not unrealistic to assume that they would invoke the powers of the Goddess as they stirred the cauldron and blessed the ingredients that were cooking inside.

Magick charms and spells were all asked of the wise woman and the cunning man and in return, a basket of eggs was given or some vegetables from the garden. Money rarely changed hands, simply because there wasn't any to spare. So goods were bartered and life went on.

Growing herbs to be used in the kitchen, spellcraft, or medicines is cheap and fun to do. They require very little looking after and once established, they almost look after themselves. Medicines involving herbs don't have to be complicated. William Coles, a celebrated herbalist wrote a book in 1656, called *The Art of Simpling*.

A 'simple' is a medicine that is made from one herb and the water it is prepared in. So if you or someone else is suffering from a sore throat, then a 'simple' can be made by boiling a bunch of basil in some water, allowing it to cool and gargling with it. Simple, but very effective, especially if the Goddess has been invoked before starting. The Goddess can be invoked before a dock leaf is picked and used to rub on the rash caused by a stinging nettle, it really is a simple as that.

Herbal medicines are effective, cheap and have very few side effects. If the Goddess is invoked in a simple ritual before the medicine is made, then its effectiveness is increased beyond measure. Blessed Be!

Dianic Witches

Most Dianic witches worship the Goddess only, and though some branches may recognise the masculine part of divinity they choose to worship the feminine side. They are exclusively female and have a feminist philosophy. Some are recognised as being primarily lesbian however there are bisexual and straight Dianic Witches. They are usually Solitaries but that might be because it's sometimes quite hard to find Dianic covens.

Gardnerian Wicca

Gerald Gardner (1883–1964) who ran a Museum of Magick and Witchcraft on the Isle of Man claimed to have been initiated in 1939 into a secret group that called themselves 'the Wica', and formed The New Forest Coven, one of England's last surviving witch covens. Witchcraft was illegal in Britain at that time, so it had to be completely secret. He wrote about his experiences with the coven in his books *Witchcraft Today* (1954) and *The Meaning of Witchcraft* (1959). He took the secrets he learned there and dedicated his life to preserving and promoting witchcraft and the resulting belief system became known as Wicca (see page 13).

He initiated a woman called Doreen Valiente (1922–1999) who became his coven's High Priestess. Doreen contributed a great deal to Gardnerian rituals and to modern Wicca itself, writing a number of books about witchcraft.

A Gardnerian is a person who has had a Gardnerian initiation administered by someone empowered to do so in a line of descent tracing back to Gerald Gardner. In Gardnerian Wicca, the two principal deities are the Horned God and the Mother Goddess. Gardnerians believe that only a witch can initiate another witch.

Alexandrian Wicca

Alexandrian Wicca is similar in many ways to Gardnerian Wicca. Founded in the sixties by Alex Sanders, who was initiated into Gardnerian Wicca, and his wife Maxine Sanders.

Some of the names and use of tools differ from Gardnerian Wicca but the distinctions between the two traditions has blurred somewhat over the years.

Sanders claimed his tradition was passed down from his grandmother. That claim was disputed by some people but it is felt by many that he made some significant contributions to the Craft.

Druids

The word Druid in Brythonic Celtic (that is, Cornish and Welsh) means either 'knowledge of the oak', and in Goidelic Celtic (that is, Irish and Scottish Gaelic), 'wise man'.

There are many different orders of modern Druids, sometimes called Neo-druids. They work with the sun and solar festivals. Other Pagan disciplines work with the moon.

Very little is known about the ancient Druids as they did not leave any written records of their existence. However, they are described in Greek and Roman writing and in medieval Irish stories. The modern Druid revival happened about 300 years ago, inspired by these stories and it reinvented Druidry for modern times.

Druids view themselves as Pagan priests. Druidry today is divided into three grades: Bard, Ovate and Druid. Bards are the storytellers, poets and musicians, they pass on knowledge and keep tradition alive through verse and writing. Ovates are mystical, they see the future, they can heal, perform magick, they are great thinkers and they must ensure the knowledge of the Druids is used only for good. Druids are teachers, counsellors and judges, they meditate and perform rituals – they have a responsibility to publicly speak out about environmental issues and injustices.

Modern Druids believe they are rekindling one of the most ancient British religions and their aim is to become at one with nature and to encourage others to be so too.

Eclectic

You could say Eclectic Witches follow 'whatever works'. Eclectic witches practise as they see fit, following whatever God, Goddess or method they choose. Many Wiccans follow a certain lineage, meaning they have been initiated into a certain tradition. Eclectic witches are not initiated and may or may not be part of a group. They freely experiment with a variety of methods. You might find them taking inspiration from Ancient Egypt, Native American religion as well as from Wiccan tradition.

The Cycles of the Moon

There is something special about moonlight and its energy. Of course it's not really light from the moon but reflected light from the sun, and its shape changes as it orbits around the earth. For a month, starting from the new moon, why not observe the changes it makes day to day?

There are four stages, or quarters, to the moon's progress. In the first quarter, the new moon is at first entirely dark then begins to appear first as a tiny sliver and grows in strength each evening. In the second quarter, we can see half of the moon and it is growing larger all the time, known as waxing. During the third quarter the moon grows in strength and beauty and becomes full. The fourth quarter is when the moon begins to reduce in size, which is known as waning.

For rituals and, eventually, spellcasting, you need to be aware of the four stages.

From New Moon to New Moon, the time it takes for the moon to orbit round the earth, the cycle is approximately a month. This is no coincidence – the period of time that we call a month was created by our ancestors to reflect this cycle.

As the new moon grows waxing and from the full moon through to the dark moon is known as waning. And so the cycle continues with, astrologically speaking, the moon spending two or so days in each planet.

Waxing Moon

Invoking rituals are carried out during the new moon to full moon (waxing) with the full moon being the best time for an invoking ritual

Waning Moon

Banishing rituals are carried out from the waning moon to the dark moon. The dark moon is the best time for banishing rituals.

The Four Stages

The Dark Moon

The side of the moon that is not illuminated by the sun faces the earth and this is called the Dark Moon. This is the first phase in the lunar cycle.

Some are uncomfortable or unsure of working at the dark of the moon but it is one of my favourite times and I consider it almost as important as the full moon. Any invoking spells or rituals can be adjusted to become banishing rituals. For instance if I was currently unemployed and had carried out a full moon ritual to have success in finding the right job, I would continue my ritual only now it would become a banishing ritual, banishing unemployment.

See if you can see a faint grey outline around the dark moon. This is the light creeping round from the other side of the moon.

1st Quarter

One day later and you'll see a tiny sliver – a waxing crescent (a growing but still concave shape). This will grow larger day by day until one week later, the moon will have completed a quarter of its orbit around the earth.

From the appearance of this first sliver of light until the moon is full is the time to perform invoking spells or rituals. This is the waxing period. When the moon is at its fullest it is at its most powerful. Most workings

are done at this time, however if there are several projects there is no harm in beginning earlier and working from the first quarter to full moon.

When the moon is new, it can be seen during the daytime, providing of course that the sky is not cloudy or overcast. Identifying the waxing or waning moon is simple. When the crescent is on the right and the tips are pointing to the left the moon is waxing. When the sliver crescent is on the left and the tips are pointing to the right the moon is waning.

Half of the moon is now illuminated by the sun. In the next few days the moon is a waxing, gibbous moon (meaning it's more than a half moon and it's now making a convex shape). To our eyes it looks like each phase lasts a few days. However, as the moon continues its orbit the shape of its illuminated surface is continually changing.

When the last phase is completed, the moon is full and visible all night, barring cloud cover.

The Full Moon

The full moon is a special time for Pagans and some sort of ceremony will be carried out.

They may simply light a candle on their work station or altar and spend a few minutes in quiet meditation or they will perform a ritual ceremony which is known as a Full Moon Esbat (page 63). Circles are cast at times of the full moon to honour the cycle of the moon, to honour the goddess or god associated with that time of year and festival, to draw down the power and energy of the moon.

'Drawing Down the Moon' (page 48) should be performed every full moon if possible.

Full moon is when the moon energy is at its most powerful stage. If you do nothing else, stand outside under the full moon and raise your arms high above your head and draw down the power and energy of the moon into your body and spirit.

Last Quarter

The final quarter, and the moon is now a waning gibbous moon. A week later and it becomes a waning crescent and finally back to its dark phase.

This is the time to perform any banishing rituals, that is, things that we want to send away, dispel, be rid of or reject. That includes negative emotions, illnesses, bad habits, and bad situations.

Void of Course

During the passage of the moon in its full cycle it passes through the signs of the Zodiac. It takes two to three days to do this and when it is not full in a sign it is called 'Void of Course'. Today, as I edit this, the moon is waxing through Gemini which is ruled by Mercury. It is right in the middle between Gemini and Cancer which is ruled by the Moon. I would consider this to be Void of Course. Tomorrow, as the moon moves more fully into Cancer, I would consider an Esbat or ritual banishing negativity (because the moon is waning) in connection with emotional family or home matters because Cancer governs the home and family and the moon governs our emotions.

To find these there are good astrology aids and calendars which are simple to use and they can be purchased online particularly from www.astrocal.co.uk

A Lunar Eclipse

A Lunar Eclipse occurs when the moon passes into the Earth's shadow and it is a very powerful, magickal and spiritual time. It does not last for very long and if it is cloudy where you live you may not even be lucky enough to see it but what a blessing it is if you do! Some like to reserve this time for meditation and reflection, others like to perform a special ritual to honour the Goddess, the choice is yours.

The Moon and the Signs of the Zodiac

As you become more aware of the movement and influence of the moon and the planets you will realise that when the moon is in particular planets or signs of the Zodiac your magick can be more focused or empowered.

There are times though, when the moon is in between two signs of the zodiac when it is known as being 'void of course' (page 28). This is not a good time to perform any kind of magick that demands a certain outcome.

The moon travels round in a cycle, which lasts a little more than twenty-eight days. During this journey, the moon passes through the twelve signs of the zodiac. It remains in each sign for a period of two to three days. It does not appear in one sign and then jump immediately to the next sign. It is a gradual process. During the short period when the moon reaches the point when it is in neither one sign nor the other, unexpected things occur and plans tend to go awry. For that reason, it is best not to perform magickal rites during these times because it is more likely to go wrong.

If you incorporate some knowledge of the qualities of the planets and the signs of the zodiac in planning your working spells you will have greater results. Being aware of the qualities of each sign will help you to choose the best time for any given ritual.

Zodiac or Sun signs are determined at our moment of birth, specifically the position of the sun at the time when we were born. Most of us know that there are twelve signs in the Zodiac. Each sign is ruled by a planet and each sign governs a particular part of the body as illustrated in Leonardo da Vinci's 'Grand Man'.

When we are performing rituals we might want to focus our attention for healing on someone who is born under the sign of Cancer. We might use the Astrological Glyph for Neptune, for healing and the glyph for Cancer for that particular person. If we were performing a healing ritual for the same person and we knew that the problem was in their knee joints we might also add the glyph for Capricorn which rules the knees. You will see now why your intention and the words that you utter are so important.

I would perhaps inscribe a candle with the glyphs mentioned above and then, when the time came during my circle, I would say something like:

Neptune mighty ruler of the seas
_____ is injured and is weak
Hear my call and hear my pleas
On his/her behalf I now speak
The pain he/she suffers is in her/his knees
Bring healing to him/her I ask of thee
Hear my call and hear my plea
An it harm none so mote it be.

Aries

Dates: 21st March–20th April
House: First
Ruler: Mars, God of War
Element: Fire
Quality: Cardinal
Symbol: The ram
Nature: Masculine
Day: Tuesday
Time: Day
Metal: Iron or steel
Gem: Bloodstone, diamond
Flowers: Poppy, roses and lilies
Colour: Red
Occupation: Politics
Governs: The head
Key word: Energy, self
Positive influences: Courage and action
Negative influences: Greed and destruction

Taurus

Dates: 21st April–20th May
House: Second
Ruler: Venus, Goddess of Love
Element: Earth
Quality: Fixed
Symbol: The bull
Nature: Feminine
Day: Friday
Time: Night
Metal: Copper
Gem: Moss agate, emerald and Beryl
Flowers: Red rose, daisy, lily, and daffodil.
Colour: Red and orange
Occupation: Economics
Governs: The ears, neck and throat
Key word: Love, possessions
Positive influences: Patience, affection and persistence
Negative influences: Stubbornness, aggression and jealousy

Gemini

Date: 21st May–21st June
Ruler: Mercury, God of Knowledge
House: Third
Element: Air
Quality: Mutable
Symbol: The twins
Nature: Masculine
Day: Wednesday
Time: Day
Metal: Quicksilver

Gem: Emerald

Flowers: Lilac, azalea and lily-of-the-valley

Colour: Orange

Occupation: Education

Governs: Hands, arms, chest and lungs

Key word: Expression, communication

Positive influences: Affection, intelligence, and astuteness.

Negative influences: Pretentiousness, shallowness and restlessness.

Cancer

Date: 22nd June–22nd July

Ruler: The Moon, Goddess of Life

House: Fourth

Element: Water

Quality: Cardinal

Symbol: The crab

Nature: Feminine

Day: Friday

Time: Night

Metal: Silver

Gem: Moonstone, ruby and pearl

Flower: Water lily, iris, white poppy, white carnation and magnolia.

Colour: Orange and yellow

Occupation: The land

Governs: The chest and stomach

Key word: Enigmatic, home

Positive influences: Self-reliant, loyal and kind

Negative influences: Unforgiving, selfish and deep.

Leo

Date 23rd July–22nd August

Ruler: The Sun, God of Life

House:Fifth

Element: Fire

Quality: Fixed

Symbol: The lion

Nature: Masculine

Day: Sunday

Time: Day

Metal: Gold

Gem: Ruby, sardonyx

Flowers: Dahlia, yellow lily, red poppy, marigold and sunflower

Colour: Yellow

Occupation: The arts

Governs: The heart

Key word: Creativity

Positive influences: Considerate, dynamic, and charming

Negative influences: Egotistic, forceful, quick tempered.

Virgo

Date: 23rd August–22nd September

Ruler: Mercury, God of Knowledge

House: Sixth

Element: Earth

Quality: Mutable

Symbol: The maiden

Nature: Feminine

Day: Wednesday

Time: Night

Metal: Quicksilver

Gem: Diamond, sapphire

Flowers Aster, chrysanthemum, ivy and fern

Colour: Yellow and green

Occupation: Public services

Governs: The digestive organs and the intestine

Key word: Expression

Positive influences: Balanced, organised and courteous

Negative influences: Negative, fretful and exacting

Libra

Date: 23rd September–22nd October

Ruler: Venus, Goddess of Love

House: Seventh

Element: Air

Quality: Cardinal

Symbol: The scales

Nature: Masculine

Day: Friday

Time: Night

Metal: Copper

Gem: Jasper, opal

Flowers: Daisies, violets, asters and orchids

Colour: Green

Occupation: Law

Governs: The loins, kidneys and back

Key word: Affection

Positive influences: Charming, refined and affectionate

Negative influences: Cutting, harsh and arrogant

Scorpio

Date: 23rd October–21st November

Ruler: Pluto, God of the Underworld, and Mars

House: Eighth

Element: Water

Quality: Fixed

Symbol: The scorpion

Nature: Feminine

Day: Tuesday

Time: Night

Metal: Plutonium

Gem: Topaz

Flowers: Anemone, heather, and gardenia.

Colour: Green and blue

Occupation: Finance

Governs: The reproductive areas

Key word: Transformation, sexuality

Positive influences: Determined, magnetic and sincere

Negative influences: Challenging, secretive and headstrong.

Ruler: Pluto, God of the Underworld

Sagittarius

Date: 22nd November–21st December

Ruler: Jupiter, God of Fortune

House: Ninth

Element: Fire

Quality: Mutable

Symbol: The archer

Nature: Masculine

Day: Thursday

Time: Day

Metal: Tin

Gem: Turquoise, ruby

Flowers: Hydrangeas, dahlias and peonies

Colour: Blue

Occupation: Travel
Governs: The thighs
Key word: Progress, philosophy
Positive influences: Adventurous, thoughtful and independent
Negative influences: Impulsive, self-centred and domineering

Capricorn
Date: 22nd December–19th January
Ruler: Saturn, God of Time
House: Tenth
Element: Earth
Quality: Cardinal
Symbol: The goat
Nature: Feminine
Day: Saturday
Time: Night
Metal: Lead
Gem: Lapis
Flowers: Camellia, orange blossom, carnation and magnolia
Colour: Deep blue
Occupation: Civil service
Governs: The knees and joints
Key word: Authority
Positive influences: Independent, refined and disciplined
Negative influences: Insecure, critical and proud

Aquarius
Date: 20th January–18th February
Ruler: Uranus, the God of Air
House: Eleventh
Element: Air
Quality: Fixed
Symbol: The water carrier
Nature: Masculine
Day: Wednesday
Time: Day
Metal: Uranium
Gem: Sapphire
Flowers: Gladioli and tiger lily
Colour: Indigo
Occupation: Parliament
Governs: The calves and ankles
Key word: Confrontation, intellect
Positive influences: Affectionate, modest and intelligent
Negative influences: Judgmental, critical and extreme

Pisces
Date: 19th February–20th March
Ruler: Neptune, God of the Sea
House: Twelfth
Element: Water
Quality: Mutable
Symbol: The fishes
Nature: Feminine
Day: Friday
Time: Night
Metal: Platinum
Gem: Pearl
Colour: Violet
Occupation: Health care
Governs: The feet
Key word: Inspiration, healing
Positive influences: Intuitive, sensitive and kind
Negative influences: Argumentative, excessive and selfish

Understanding the Twelve Moons

January the Wolf Moon

In Native American tradition, 'Wolf' is the teacher of the tribe and shows wisdom to the wolf pack. Wolf is my totem (emblem) and I am particularly fond of this animal and all it stands for.

Esbats at this time would be for family and friends for their protection and wisdom. This is a time to make sure that your 'tribe' – close friends and family – are well, healthy, and happy and have all they need. If one of yours is experiencing any kind of difficulty then now would be a good time to carry out a ritual asking the Lord and Lady for blessings for those that you care for. You can also ask for blessings for people that you don't know, such as those in other countries who are experiencing hardship for whatever reason. As the moon is waning, or at the Dark Moon, carry out a spell or ritual to banish negativity.

Also known as the Cold Moon, January is named after Janus, the Roman God of doors and gates.

February the Storm Moon

Still in the grip of winter, in days gone by people would have prepared for February by having jams and preserves stored from the summer crops and they would still have root vegetables to sustain them, but supplies would be running low and everyone would have to be careful. In today's society fortunately (or unfortunately) we have supermarkets nearby so we can pick up the things we need.

You need food to sustain your body but your spirit needs sustenance too. On this Esbat you should be thinking about purification, meditation and healing and begin to make lists for new plans that will begin soon.

Don't forget about your garden. This would be a good time to think about what you will plant and where you will plant it. Remember, plants that give bounty over the ground should be planted when the moon is rising, such as peas and tomatoes whilst root vegetables should be planted during the waning moon

February is also known as the Quickening Moon and is named after

Februus, a minor god of death and purification. Februa is the Roman festival of purification, and a time to make sacrifices and to atone for sins.

March the Chaste Moon

March comes in like a breath of fresh air and we can begin to see signs of life in the garden. It will still be fairly cold but there is an air of eager anticipation for the new beginnings ahead and people generally look happier. This Esbat you should be thinking about growth and development of the plans that have been put into place and rituals could be for success for these plans and for gratitude too that we have survived the cold winter. March is named after Mars, the Roman God of war.

April the Seed Moon

Just as the seeds you have planted in your garden, window boxes or plant pots begin to sprout so too do your ideas and plans begin to become a reality. This is a positive time and you should make the most of it. Show gratitude in your Esbat and give thanks for every living thing.

April is named after Aprillis the Latin name which comes from Aphrodite the Greek Goddess of love and beauty, whom the Romans knew as the Goddess Venus. This then is a perfect time to think also about friendships, love and beauty and a perfect Esbat for glamorising (beauty) rituals but the Goddess likes to see you making an effort too so dedicate the first weeks of the new moon to yourself and to pampering your body.

May the Flower Moon

Named after Maia, the Goddess of growth of plants, May is also the time of the Hare Moon. The Hare is a Magickal creature who would have been briefly seen in March as the Mad March Hare Dancing and cavorting in the moonlight. Kit Berry's series of books on Stonewylde feature the hare in its magickal splendour dancing under the full of the moon with the Moongazy girl Sylvie, and the month of May is a perfect time to do just that; dance in the full of the moon and delight in your own beauty. Give thanks during this Esbat for the wonderful world that you live in.

June the Mead Moon

June is named after the Roman Goddess Juno, identified with the Greek Goddess Hera who is celebrated on the 2nd of June. She is the Goddess of marriage and the well-being of women. This is a very special time for Martin and I as we were hand fasted on this date.

This month is sometimes known as the Honey Moon. Perhaps that's where we get the term honeymoon with so many handfastings from Beltane onwards. This Esbat is a good time for Fertility rituals and for protection too so that we all have a good harvest, strengthening rituals would be helpful at this time so that our nursing mothers and those about to be nursing mothers, our crops, and our plans have the best opportunity for success.

July the Hay Moon

We are right in the middle here, looking back over achievements and forward to additional accomplishments and to preparation for the next winter. During this Esbat we could be performing rituals for gratitude for those blessings that we have already received and for prosperity, abundance, success, power, wisdom and victory. The summertime brings in travel too with people going on holiday and old friends coming to visit us so travel and friendship rituals could be performed also. July is named after the Roman Emperor Julius Caesar.

August the Corn Moon

Named after the second great Roman Emperor Augustus Caesar who was also regarded as a God, August is also known as the Grain Moon. During this month we reap what we have sown in more ways than one. Some of our plans and actions will have borne fruit whilst others may have developed in a different manner from which they were intended. Some of our plants may have taken very well and produced a good harvest whilst others may have faltered and failed. At this Esbat we should reflect on what has gone before and see where we can improve for there is still time to make the best of what we have. As always we should show gratitude for what we have received and pray for that which is still to come and this should be reflected in our Esbat rituals.

September the Harvest Moon

Also known as the Wine Moon September is a time of thanksgiving and balance. Perhaps these words have a double meaning for if we are making wine then there is a danger that we will be overindulgent and lose our balance so we must be aware in everything that we do that the world works in balance and harmony like white and black, night and day, light and dark yin and yang. This is a spiritual period where again we reflect on what has gone before and look ahead and inwards in meditation and visualisation.

We should already be thinking of winter and making preparations for that which may lie ahead of us.

October the Blood Moon

Known by many other names such as Hunter's Moon, and Traveller's Moon the Blood Moon was probably named after the blood that was shed from slaughtering animals for curing to see us through the winter so we give thanks this Esbat in remembrance of all who have passed whether they have done so in protecting others, working to feed, clothe or house others and for living things that have been sacrificed to feed us.

Giving thanks is essential at every Esbat, but at this one we should give thanks to those who have died for us in past and present conflicts. Many men have sacrificed their lives for us. Wives go without husbands, mothers go without sons, and children go without fathers. Women have been lost in conflict too and the pain for their loved ones is just as traumatic. At this Esbat we should think of all those who have suffered at our expense and remember them for the price that they have paid is far too great.

November the Snow Moon

Winter has arrived and although we may not have snow on the ground it will be very cold outside. Mother Earth is now at rest, she has worked hard throughout the spring and summer and borne the fruits of her labour for us to enjoy. We too have worked hard in many different ways and we too should be prepared to take things a little easier. The days are shorter and the nights are longer so we should conserve our energy and concentrate on those tasks that can be done indoors. Esbats at this time should be done for health and healing, protection and spirituality.

December the Oak Moon

This is a time when we prepare for celebration and reunions. Families and friends get together and in past times people would have saved some of their valuable food stores so that they could have a special treat on this occasion. Winter is coming to an end and soon very soon spring will arrive once more, completing the Wheel of the Year.

During this month, Esbats would be for safe travel for those friends or family members making a long winter journey to reunite with loved ones, for protection and of course for gratitude, always show gratitude, and remembrance for those who can no longer be with us at this very special time.

Blue Moons

There are only twelve full moons in each year, one appearing every month. On very rare occasions, a Blue Moon will occur making thirteen full moons in that year, hence the expression 'Once in a Blue Moon'. The first moon in that month is a standard full moon however the second full moon in the same month is a Blue Moon. This is a very powerful moon and a very powerful month. The table below shows the Blue moons that have occurred since 2001 and that will occur until the year 2028.

Year	Month	Day	Time
2001	November	30	20:50
2004	July	31	18:06
2007	June	30	13:49
2009	December	31	19:13
2012	August	31	13:59
2015	July	31	10:44
2018	January	31	13:27
2018	March	31	12:37
2020	October	31	14:50
2023	August	31	1:36
2026	May	31	8:46
2028	December	31	16:49

The Planets

You do not have to be an astrologer to perform rituals or spells or magickal workings, however, using an astro-calendar will give you enough insight to be able to plan and work in harmony with the planets, and the Zodiac. The following explanations may help you to understand a little more and empower your rituals.

The Moon

The moon governs our feelings and emotions and our ability to respond to everyday affairs.
Key words: feelings, moods, instincts, habits, reflections, sensitivity, depression, sentimentality, nurturing aspirations, fluctuations.
Day of the week: Monday.

Sun

The Sun governs our personality, our vitality, and our creative self expression.
Key words: the father, royalty, nobility, leadership, power, government, life, will, ego, vitality, confidence, success, intellect, wisdom, fame and wealth.
Day of the week: Sunday.

Jupiter

Jupiter governs social, cultural, religious and educational values.
Key words: mentality, wisdom, prophecy, religion, education, law, abundance, philosophy, optimism, prosperity, generosity, joviality, fortune, optimism, finance, commerce, good luck, success, expansion, growth, opportunity, confidence, wisdom, optimism and generosity.
Day of the week: Thursday.

Venus

Venus governs our social, romantic, and artistic abilities.
Key words: happiness, love, creativity, balance, peace, harmony, diplomacy,

cooperation, beauty, nature, affection, pleasure, charm, friendship, wealth, romance, passion, music, marriage and unions.
Day of the week: Friday.

Mars

Mars governs our capacity for action and personal desires.
Key words: adventure, innovation, enthusiasm, impulsiveness, active, passion, war, violence, quarrels, accidents, energy, drive and leadership.
Day of the week: Tuesday.

Mercury

Mercury governs our mind and mental abilities.
Key words: speed, communication, media, inventiveness, curiosity, restlessness, creativity, movement, education, logic, fickle, education, writers and businessmen.
Day of the week: Wednesday.

Saturn

Saturn governs our capacity for organisation, work, self-discipline and serious issues.
Key words: organisation structure caution poverty conservatism pessimism depression realism stagnation restriction misfortune ambition perseverance status politics authority discipline seriousness, caution economy, melancholy, reserve taciturnity, segregation and seclusion, calcification, old age, agriculture, mining and property.
Day of the week: Any.

Uranus

Uranus governs our ability for original self-expression and the search for new experience.
Key words: freedom, truth, awareness, change, disruptive, enlightenment, genius, revelations, awakenings, alchemy, astrology, science, innovation,

suddenness, revolution, transmutation, independence, excitability, impulsiveness, innovators, reformers, inventors, technicians; magicians and astrologers.
Day of the week: Saturday.

Neptune

Neptune governs our imaginative spiritual and intuitive faculties.
Key words: higher consciousness, destiny, illusion, mystical, imaginative, equality, compassion, kindness, humanitarianism, hospitals, healing, prisons, subtlety, confusion, delusion, deception, escapism, surreal, sensitive, intuitive, religious, impressionability, fantasy, imagination, mysticism, vagueness, confusion and deception
Day of the week: Any.

Pluto

Pluto governs our ability for change elimination and renewal.
Key words: change, elimination, renewal, creation, destruction, courage, destruction, rebuilding, sexuality, fertility, providence, power, will, influence propagandists, politicians, actors and orators.
Day of the week: Any.

The Wiccan Rede

The Wiccan Rede is a statement that sums up the philosophy behind Wicca. In its simplest form – though you'll see it in several variations – the Wiccan Rede is:

'An it harm none, do what ye will'.

    Meaning if it harms no one then do as you please.

    'An' is not a shortened form of 'and' but an archaic English word meaning 'if'.

    The premise is centuries old – and not primarily confined to Pagan teachings (you'll find the same thoughts put forth by John Stuart Mill and St Augustin of Hippo) – but the actual words themselves pertaining to a Wiccan way of life were written down in modern times, though the date is unclear. Possibly early in the 20th century.

'Eight words the Wiccan Rede fulfil, An it harm none, Do what ye will.'

    These words are from the poem *The Wiccan Rede* which has been attributed to Adriana Porter (1857–1946), grandmother of Lady Gwen Thompson (1928 –1986). There is also a poem by Doreen Valiente (1922–1999), who some call the mother of modern witchcraft, called *The Wiccan Rede* which has a similar line to the one above and some Wiccans recite this during rituals.

    Whenever the Wiccan Rede was written, it's the sentiment that is important. The rede observes 'The Threefold Rule', namely that whatever you put out will come back to you three times.

    There is no right or wrong way to follow a Pagan path unless you are a member of a specific coven which will have its own rules or disciplines. What is important is that you remember whatever you put out will come back to you threefold. In short what this means is that you can do whatever you like but if you harm another by design or intention that same harm will come back to you multiplied by three. Equally, in acts of goodness or kindness these acts will be repaid in triplicate.

    This is probably derived from the triple Goddess, the Maiden, the Mother, and the Crone. If you please or displease one you please or displease all three.

The Wiccan Rede poem is recited by some Wiccans when casting a circle but I think it is nice to compose your own verse for your own rituals. Below is my version of the Rede and of course you are very welcome to use that but, if you are inspired to do so, why not write your own.

Soraya's Rede

Follow her in perfect love
In honour truth and perfect trust.

Obey her laws on every day
Be true to her in every way.

My circle's cast for all to see
Let none enter who should not be.

Around I go, times one, two, three.
Full moon above it watches me.

Deosil the circle cast
Rituals set true to last.

But in the dark to banish all
Widdershins it is my call.

By Lady's light I heed the rule
And do no harm by any tool.

I do to you as you to me
Lest bad return to me by three.

These words the Wiccan Rede fulfil
An it harm none, do as you will.

Casting a Circle

Most rituals take place within a magick or sacred circle. Whilst working within the circle we are between this world and the astral world. It can be likened to meditating.

Purpose

Casting a circle serves several purposes such as:—

- To contain the powerful energy with which we will be working.
- To keep out and protect us from negative energy.
- To focus our minds and our intentions.
- To welcome the Lady and Lord into our sacred space.

The Four Quarters

The four quarters relate to the directions, to the elements and to the seasons.

East (where the sun rises) relates to the element of Air and is the beginning of new ideas or plans.

South is the element of Fire and brings new ideas to life.

West (where the sun sets) is the element of Water which nourishes these ideas or plans and helps them to grow and develop.

North is the element of Earth which gives theses plans a strong foundation.

To begin with, that is all you have to know to start casting your first circle and you should not be attempting any kind of magick at this stage.

The first time that you cast a circle you will probably be filled with all sorts of insecurities, so it is important that your first few circles are practice runs so that you can be familiar with everything that you need and then you can be confident in your work instead of insecure.

But, and this is the biggest but, your most important question should be 'Why am I casting a circle?'.

There are many reasons for casting a circle and you will not and should not be spell-casting every time you are 'working in circle'.

Reasons for Casting a Circle (Intent)

The first reason to cast a circle is to honour the God and the Goddess at the eight Pagan festivals. These eight festivals mark the changing seasons and were important in past times because we all depended on the land and its produce to survive. Knowing the seasons was and still is important to survival.

Think for a moment what your life would be like if there were no supermarkets or shops and how you would eat without an easily available supply. The land is our source of food whether you eat meat or are vegetarian it makes no difference. Our vegetables are grown in the earth and our animals eat what is grown in the earth. Without some knowledge of when and how to plant we would not survive. In ancient times our ancestors appreciated the value of the land and the effect the changing seasons had on the success or failure of our crops. They respected the power of the elements and gave worship to the Gods and Goddesses who governed each season. In today's society we tend to 'worship' retail outlets and don't give a thought to where things actually come from.

Preparation

In traditional circle casting, a broom would be used to sweep round the circle, sweeping it clean.

This circle should have four quarters. The first quarter is the east, the second quarter is south, the third quarter is west and the fourth quarter is north. You mark these out with candles. You could also use crystals to help mark out the circle. Rinse any crystals in clean water to cleanse them.

Prepare yourself as you would for any other important event in your life. You can start with a warm bath with essential oils to prepare your mood. My favourites for any kind of spiritual work are marjoram and frankincense.

Lay out the clothes that you have decided to wear and any jewellery that has special meaning to you.

Place all your magickal tools on your altar and set your quarter candles in place.

True magick begins in your mind by using your mind to create change. That is the most important thing to remember here.

However, I can make an ordinary meal and enjoy it well enough. But I can also invite friends to dinner and create something really special. I might spend days planning a special menu and buying the ingredients. I would use nice tableware, buy some good wine and choose some suitable music to play. On the day of the meal I would make sure that my home was cleaned from top to bottom and I would prepare the food for my guests. Finally, I would have a nice bath; fix my hair, put on my makeup and a lovely outfit ready to greet my guests.

In the same way, when casting a circle, sometimes all I have to do is focus my mind and visualise my circle around me or perform a simple ceremony but on other occasions I am able to prepare for something grander.

Remember, being a Pagan is not just about performing spells. Being a Pagan is a way of life. It is a Goddess-based belief system where you respect the Moon, the Sun, the Earth, the Sea, the Seasons, indeed everything above, around, and on the earth.

I believe that all the Gods and Goddesses are merely facets of one God/dess who is both feminine and masculine. Pagans show their respect for Goddesses and Gods and have particular favourites but also address individual aspects of particular Goddesses or Gods at different times depending on the time of year or where the planets are or what they are trying to achieve. Whether you cast your circle mentally or physically the purpose for casting it remains the same.

When:
Decide when you are going to perform your ritual. It may be:-
* A Sabbat to honour a particular festival.
* A Full Moon Esbat to honour the Goddess.
* An Esbat (a ceremony that is carried out before the moon is full) for a particular ritual or spell.
* A Waning Moon Banishing ritual.
* A Dark Moon Ritual.

Where:
Decide where you are going to perform your ritual. It may be:
* Outside: prepare and mark out the area with stones, crystals or flowers
* Inside: clean the room as though you were welcoming an important guest. I work inside in a small room and consider the whole of it as my circle.
* The altar: Set up your altar gathering the main tools that you will use.
* On the right side of you altar place the censor, wand, athame, boline, a bowl of salt and a picture or statue of the God

- On the left side of your altar place the cup or chalice, the pentacle, bell, crystal, bowl of water and a statue or picture of the Goddess.

Tools:
- The broom and the cauldron can be on the floor to the left of the altar. I happen to have a small tabletop cauldron which I use to hold the water.
- A bell.
- Place a Pillar or Goddess candle on the altar.
- Place four tea light candles at the four quarters starting at the east.
- A lighter or matches and a small container to hold spent matches.
- Paper and pen (if you need them).
- Candles for candle magick
- Cords for cord or knot magick
- Some magickal components for whatever spell or ritual you are working on.

Magickal Components

There are numerous components that can be used to empower or symbolise your intentions during your ritual or spell casting work. The list is not all you can use, you may have other ideas, and providing you think carefully about what these items mean to you and your intentions, you can use whatever you like. Remember just because something is on the list does not mean that you have to use it. For example you may use a key for a property ritual whilst someone else may consider a key as a symbol to find answers or for new opportunities. The magickal components list (page 132) is made up of suggestions only:

- Photographs of couples for romance rituals
- Photographs or ornaments of animals to symbolise protection, peace prosperity etc
- Keys or schedules for property rituals,
- Tarot cards to symbolise signs of the zodiac or situations
- Essential oils or blends to empower or honour
- Herbs to empower or honour.
- Crystals to empower or honour.

The list could be endless and you could get really bogged down and confused. Remember, keep it simple, and perhaps just use one thing that you have to hand to symbolise your intention rather than trying to use everything. See page 132 for my list of possible magickal components.

When you have prepared everything you can begin to prepare yourself. Decide what you will be wearing and have a nice bath or shower and as you are doing so think about the ritual that you will be performing. Prepare your mind as well as your body.

Drawing Down The Moon

Drawing down the moon should be performed every full moon, even though the sky may be overcast and the moon invisible to you. Stand outside if possible but if the weather is severe and you cannot do this outside then stand near a window. Cast your circle in the usual way and at the appropriate time, raise your arms high above your head, and say a prayer to the Goddess or use a Goddess invocation that you are familiar with. Feel the energy flowing into your body. Feel the Goddess energy empowering you. From that point forward you can carry out and magickal workings. Cast your circle in the usual way (up until point 12 on page 51).

What we are really doing here is drawing on the energy of the moon to bring our energy into contact with the energy of the Moon Goddess, restoring our vitality and strengthening our purpose.

Casting a Circle

1 Preparation
Sweep the area symbolically using your broom, sweeping outwards from the centre. Place your quarter candles in the east, west, south and north of your circle and your altar.

2 Contemplation
Sit or stand before your altar and spend some quiet time preparing and settling your mind.

Ring your bell three times.

3 Light the quarter candles

Light the four quarter candles using the appropriate salutation of your choice starting from the east, then west, then south and then north.

Once this has been done, stand at the edge of your circle and visualise white light pouring into it from infinity above. Focus your mind on the source of infinity above you, Father God, and the strength of the earth beneath your feet, Mother Earth. Prepare yourself spiritually and mentally and think of your intentions. Visualise a temple of light and love growing over your circle. When you are ready, say these words.

The circle is about to be cast and the temple erected.
Let the light and the love and the energy which fills my sacred space be pure and work for the highest good and harm none.

4 Draw the circle

Using your sword, athame, wand or finger draw the complete circle line starting at the east. Replace your instrument on the altar.

5 Cut a doorway

Cut the shape of a doorway between the North and the East (if possible) in case you have to leave your circle. Don't worry if you forget as you can always cut and open (symbolically) at any given time if you should need to.

6 Light your incense

Light you incense or censer (air/east). Bless it using the appropriate words of your choice such as these:

I bless this censer to purify, cleanse and protect my circle.

Walk round the outer edge of the circle allowing the smoke to swirl the edges, starting at the east and then say:

I bless the east with this sacred scent to purify, cleanse and protect my circle.
I bless the south with this sacred scent to purify, cleanse and protect my circle.
I bless the west with this sacred scent to purify, cleanse and protect my circle.
I bless the north with this sacred scent to purify, cleanse and protect my circle.

Move to the east to complete the circle and then return to the centre of your circle and place your incense on the altar.

7 Light your altar candles
Enter your circle and walk to the altar, and, taking your lighter or matches, light first the large white altar candle then the large black altar candle and lastly the dinner candle. Remove the dinner candle from its holder and move to the east of your circle. Light the east candle from the dinner candle.

8 Place your finger in the water
Place your finger in the dish of water (water/west) and bless it using the appropriate words of your choice then sprinkle a little water round the outer edge of the circle starting at the east. Replace the water dish on the altar.

Let this water purify my body and spirit that I may use it for the highest good.

9 Place your finger in the salt
Place your finger in the container of salt (earth/north) and bless it using the appropriate words of your choice then sprinkle a little salt round the outer edge of the circle starting at the east. Replace the dish of salt on the altar

Let this salt of life purify my body and spirit that I may use it for the highest good.

10 Sprinkle salt and water round your circle
Place three pinches of salt into the water and stir it clockwise three times.
   Return to the east rim of your circle and begin to sprinkle the salt and water round the edge of your circle saying as you do so:

I bless the east with salt and water to purify, cleanse and protect my circle.
I bless the south with salt and water to purify, cleanse and protect my circle.
I bless the west with salt and water to purify, cleanse and protect my circle.
I bless the north with salt and water to purify, cleanse and protect my circle.

Move to the east to complete the circle and then return to your altar. Place your dish on the altar.

Ring the bell three times.

11 Call the guardians of the four watchtowers

Call the guardians of the four watchtowers starting at the east using the appropriate words of your choice and draw a pentacle in the air at each quarter as you do so.

May the watchtower of the east, element of air, guard and protect this sacred space and grant me the blessings I require to fulfil my desires so that they harm none.
May the watchtower of the south, element of fire, guard and protect this sacred space and grant me the blessings I require to fulfil my desires so that they harm none.
May the watchtower of the west, element of water, guard and protect this sacred space and grant me the blessings I require to fulfil my desires so that they harm none.
May the watchtower of the north, element of earth, guard and protect this sacred space and grant me the blessings I require to fulfil my desires so that they harm none.

Move to the east to complete the circle and then return to your altar and draw an invoking pentacle above you.

Ring the bell three times.

12 Invoke the Goddess = Drawing Down the Moon

Invoke the Goddess by Drawing Down the Moon or the energy.

Open your arms wide, raise your hands high above your head, focus all your attention on the moon above you, and visualise the Goddess sending down her light and love to you.

Draw this energy into your heart, into your spirit and into your body. Give thanks for those blessings that you have already received, your health, your career, your family and your loved ones. Lower your arms and extend them out by your sides saying:

I call upon the Goddess to ask for assistance with my task.
May she be ever-present in my work and in my life.
I am grateful for those gifts and blessings that I have already been given and I am open and ready to receive those that are waiting to come to me.

Pick up a cup of juice, wine or water and hold it high above your head allowing the energy and the blessings of the moon to charge this liquid. Place the cup on the table, raise the second athame or crystal wand high above your head, and allow the energy and the blessings of the moon to charge it too. Now lower the athame or crystal wand into the cup to symbolise the joining of male and female aspects of deity, of man and of life. Say these words:

May man and woman be joined for eternal joy and happiness. May the plants that sustain us be fruitful and may we all be blessed with abundance.

Remove the athame from the cup and lay it to one side.

Your circle is now fully charged and you are ready to begin whatever task you have chosen to do.

Ring the bell three times

13 Meditate, pray, spellcast
Sit or kneel at your altar and carry out any prayers, meditations, purify your ritual accessories, spell casting or other work as is your intention.

When you are finished ring the bell three times.

14 Give water and salt back to the earth
When you have finished, give the water and salt back to the earth by pouring it into the ground just before you close your circle. If you are working inside your home, you can save this until you have finished and then go outside and pour this sacred liquid on to the soil in your circle or special place.

15 Thank the Lady and Lord
Before you close your circle thank the Lady and Lord for their presence and begin to end the ritual. Say these words (or invent your own):

Lord and Lady thank you for assisting me with my tasks. We have met in love and friendship, let us part the same way. May the love that has been in this circle be shared with all. Merry we meet, merry we part, merry may we meet again.

16 Thank the four watchtowers

Before you close your circle, thank the four watchtowers starting with the east say these words:

The temple will now be closed.

May the watchtower of the east, element of air take for your use any powers that have not been used.

May the watchtower of the south, element of fire, take for your use any powers that have not been used.

May the watchtower of the west, element of water, take for your use any powers that have not been used.

May the watchtower of the north, element of earth, take for your use any powers that have not been used.

And it harm none so mote it be.

17 Go back to the centre of your circle.

Go back to the centre of your circle and begin to clean and clear away your magickal tools.

Take the incense stick and touch it to the liquid to put it out and give thanks to the element of air for its blessings.

If you are outside, you can give the sacred liquid back to the earth by pouring it on the ground. If you are not put it aside and do this later. As you do so give thanks to the elements of water and earth for their blessings.

Using a candle snuffer, put out the candles on your altar and, as you do so, give thanks to the element of fire for its blessings.

Move to the edge of your circle and, using the candle snuff, put out your candles, one by one, starting at the east quarter, then the south, the west and lastly the north.

Thank your athame for guarding the entrance to your sacred space, and place it with the rest of your tools.

18 The circle is now closed.

Purifying and Consecrating your Ritual Accessories

Initially you will cast a circle to communicate with the Goddess and give thanks to her for bringing you to this point in your life. You may also want to use the first occasion to purify and consecrate all your ritual jewellery and accessories.

Cast your circle in the way shown. When you reach point 12, after you have rung the bell three times, you can bless your altar tools or ritual jewellery or anything else that requires attention. This is easily done. Prepare some consecrated water using the purification verse.

Salt is life, here is life,
Sacred be without strife.
Salt is life, here is life,
Sacred be without strife.
Salt is life, here is life,
Blessed be without strife.

Once this is done, hold each tool, piece of jewellery or other item high above your head and name it in the fashion of:

This is my athame

Wet your hands with the consecrated water and stroke the item that you are blessing. You could say something like the verse below or use other appropriate words of your choice:

Bless it clean, bless it pure,
Make its purpose true and sure.
Vibrations dark do send away
Keep pure and light from this day.

You can do the same thing with your altar and any clothes or items that you work with.

Casting the Circle — Summary

1   Enter your circle. Sweep the area using your broom.
2   Sit or stand before your altar.
    Ring your bell three times.
3   Light the four quarter candles.
4   Using your athame draw the complete circle.
5   Cut the shape of a doorway between the north and the east.
6   Light your incense.
7   Light the altar candle (fire/south)
8   Place your finger in the dish of water (water/west).
9   Place your finger in the container of salt (earth/north)
10 Sprinkle a little salt round the outer edge of the circle starting at the east. Replace the dish of salt on the altar
    Ring the bell three times.
11 Call the guardians of the four watchtowers starting at the east using the appropriate words of your choice and drawn a pentacle in the air at each quarter as you do so.
12 Invoke the Goddess by drawing down the moon or the energy.
    Draw an invoking pentacle in the air high above your head.
    Ring the bell three times.
13 Carry out any prayers, meditations spell casting or other work When you are finished ring the bell three times.
14 Give water and salt back to the earth.
15 Thank the Lady and Lord for their presence and begin to close end the ritual.
16 Thank the four watchtowers starting with the east
17 Go back to the centre of your circle
18 The circle is now closed

Initiations

Initiation = Solitary

You may actually realise that you are a Wiccan or Pagan after you have been behaving in a manner typical of a follower of the old ways. This can almost be like an awakening or a realisation that comes from reading or seeing something and suddenly you realise that you have, without knowing it, been doing or living in this fashion for some time.

You might have felt drawn by the power of the full moon and found yourself needing to go outside or stand at your window and gaze upon her beauty. You may have been meditating on things that you have wished to happen in your future and then been surprised that they have actually happened. You may have empowered your visualisation by writing these wishes down. But one day when the time is right you will feel the need to go further.

You may at this time not really feel comfortable about joining a coven and indeed may not even be aware of any in your area. If and when you reach that stage and wish to perform some sort of ritual or ceremony then a self-dedication or initiation ceremony would be perfect to begin with.

This is a very personal moment in time for you and it marks the true beginning of your journey. From this point onwards you will probably begin to look out for Pagan books, you may already have done this, and have started to gather together some of the 'accessories' that you need. You may in fact have nothing more than a few candles. That is not a problem, as part of the excitement is finding the very things that you are looking for. You may find that you already have some in your home. I found some of my Pagan tools at home, and in second hand or antique shops and some of them I purchased new. Either is acceptable although some would say that your tools have to be new so that the energy is pure. But how can that be when the chances are that you won't have known who made them and in what circumstances they were made in the first place? Whether they are old or new is not important as you will consecrate or bless, purify or dedicate your tools for your ritual purposes and you may already have done this. More important is your magickal name and great care should be taken in choosing it (page 111).

Initiation with a Coven

Whilst some covens may have as many as five levels of initiation, most have three. At first and second degree they are referred to as priestesses or priests. At third degree, couples who work together may choose to branch out to begin their own covens and at that point they become High Priestess and High Priest of their new coven and the High Priestess of the coven they have left becomes a Queen. If they remain with their existing coven they may be known as Elders.

Prior to taking the First Degree a student will most likely be know as an Initiate. To begin with, students of the craft would be required to study for a period of at least one year and one day before being initiated to First Degree. During this study period they may be expected to:-

- Choose or find a magickal name
- Attend regular training sessions
- Perform various exercises
- Attend the coven's rituals on a regular basis.
- Observe and participate if required to
- Create their own Book of Shadows
- Learn and Practice visualisations, meditations, and grounding exercises
- Learn Coven, Craft and Circle customs and etiquette
- Learn the basics of a ritual
- Learn and understand the wheel of the year
- Learn and understand divination
- Learn and understand elemental correspondences
- Acquire a basic set of magickal tools and become familiar with their uses.
- Learn and understand magickal theory and practice
- Learn and understand circle casting and opening
- Learn and understand cleansing and blessing techniques
- Learn and understand how to set up an altar

First Degree

The first degree initiation is a powerful and profound ceremony carried out by the High Priestess and the High Priest in front of the coven and before embarking on this step it is essential that the student has complete and total trust in the High Priestess, High Priest, and members of the coven. The one year and one day study period help the student and coven members to get to know and trust each other and develop a strong bond of sister and brotherhood. As with all other aspect of Wicca the 1st Degree Initiation will vary from coven to coven. When the student has achieved the 1st degree level they will then begin to study for another period of one year and one day although this time may vary from coven to coven.

Self=dedication Ceremony for Solitaries

Gather together all the things that you will need on your altar: tall candles and holders, four small tea light candles for the four quarters, matches, salt, water, an athame or wand, small dishes of anointing oil that you can make yourself.

It is more important that your mind is focused on your intention and that your intention is honourable and does not interfere with another person's will. Your thoughts must be pure and sincere and your wishes should be for positive reasons rather than negative ones. You must remember that whatever you put out will come back to you threefold.

When you have gathered together all the items that you are going to use and you have prepared yourself and your surroundings you may move on to the next step.

Four small white candles should be placed at each corner of your room and this should be done starting at the East, (element of air) then the South (element of fire) then the West, (element of water) and then the North (element of earth). If you are unsure of the directions and do not have a compass then remember that the sun rises in the east and sets in the west. If you are still unsure then place your east candle to your left as you enter your room.

Sit or kneel comfortably in front of your table or altar. Close your eyes and as you breathe in, picture positive white light energy filling your body. As you breathe out, breathe away all negative energy. After some minutes, you will feel all tension flowing away from your mind and body. Allow pure light energy to flow into and through your entire body filling your sacred space, filling your room. When you are completely relaxed, stand up and move quietly to the east quarter of your room.

Ring a bell three times or use chimes if you have them to signal the start of your ceremony.

Starting with the east to the south, the west, and the north, light the four tea light candles.

Return to the centre and begin to cast the circle line using your wand, athame, sword or finger.

Start at the east, saying:

This circle line I now prepare,
Let no one enter should they dare.
This sacred space I dedicate,
Filled with love and never hate.
So mote it be.

Symbolically cut the shape of a doorway then return to the centre and replace any tool that you have used on the Altar.

Now take a smudge stick or incense stick, light it and allow the smoke to develop and begin to walk round the perimeter of your circle blessing each quarter with the element of Air.

Hail to the East Element of Air.
Hail to the South Element of Fire.
Hail to the West Element of Water.
Hail to the North Element of Earth.

Return to the centre, light the altar candle and take it to the east walking clockwise (deosil) round the perimeter of your circle. As you go bless each quarter with appropriate words of your choice or repeat:

Hail to the East Element of Air.
Hail to the South Element of Fire.
Hail to the West Element of Water.
Hail to the North Element of Earth.

Return to the centre and take three pinches of salt and add them to your dish of water. Raise your dominant hand high above you and feel the energy of the Goddess. When you feel ready put your index finger into the water stirring clockwise as you say:

Salt is life, here is life. Sacred be without strife.
Salt is life, here is life. Sacred be without strife.
Salt is life, here is life. Blessed be without strife.

Take your dish of consecrated water and move to the east walking round your circle clockwise and sprinkling the consecrated water as you go while saying appropriate words of your choice or repeat:

Hail to the East Element of Air.
Hail to the South Element of Fire.
Hail to the West Element of Water.
Hail to the North Element of Earth.

Return to the altar and replace the consecrated water and pick up the dish of salt. Move to the east and begin to sprinkle a little salt round the perimeter of your circle saying the appropriate words of your choice or repeat:

Hail to the East Element of Air.
Hail to the South Element of Fire.
Hail to the West Element of Water.
Hail to the North Element of Earth.

Move quietly back to your work space replace the dish of salt and ring the bell three times. Raise your arms high above your head and say:

I call upon the Guardians of the four watchtowers. May they stand in strength ever watchful over my circle.

Starting at the east make the sign of the pentacle saying:

Hail Guardian of the East come bless my space with light and air.

Then the south:

Hail Guardian of the South come bless my space with light and fire.

Then the west:

Hail Guardian of the West come bless my space with light and water.

Then the North:

Hail Guardian of the north come bless my space with light and earth

Make the sign of the pentacle above your head and on the ground in front of you.

Raise your arms high above your head and say:

I call upon the Lord and the Lady to enter into this sacred space and witness my rite.

Return to your altar and take your white candle. Raise it high and say:

By candle light I make my vow
The Old Ways forever from now
It is my will for all to see
Let it harm none so mote it be!

Before the God and Goddess, I (your name), henceforth wish to be known as (your craft name), within the circle of the wise to symbolise my rebirth. I pledge to honour the God and the Goddess in all areas of my life. I will work in harmony with the energies of the Earth, showing respect for Plant, Animal, Spirit, and Man, striving always for unity and balance. I will honour and respect my brothers and sisters in the Craft even when our paths do not join. I will respect and keep the Old Ways and the Wiccan Rede. So mote it be.

Take your anointing oil and put a little on your index finger and make the sign of the pentacle on your forehead, on your throat, on your heart and on the palms of both hands. Spend some time meditating on your life and the changes that you are making – when you are finished you may close your circle saying.

This circle is now closed, yet the work goes on. I thank the Lord and The Lady for witnessing my rite, may the energies gathered here disperse and return to the earth.

Extinguish the East candle saying:

Take for your use any powers of air that have not been used.

Extinguish the South candle:

Take for your use any powers of fire that have not been used.
Extinguish the West candle:
Take for your use any powers of water that have not been used.

Extinguish the North candle:

Take for your use any powers of earth that have not been used.

Esbats

Esbats are minor celebrations carried out any time from waxing to full moon, and waning to new moon. A full moon is the most common time to have an Esbat and it is the most powerful time for any magickal or ritual workings. Esbats are dedicated to the Goddess.

Many covens meet to coincide with the full moon to work magick, blessings or to give thanks. Solitaries can use this time to meditate and pray and make or purify magickal items.

As a rule of thumb, invoking (creating or welcoming) spells would be carried out from the first quarter to the full moon when the moon is waxing, and banishing (sending away) spells would be carried out from the first day after the full moon to the dark moon, when the moon is waning.

In short any spell can be done at any time; for instance a spell for money, prosperity, or financial gain would be invoked at the time of the waxing moon. Yet a spell to banish poverty could be carried out during the waning or dark moon. Just as invoking spells are at there most powerful at the full of the moon, so too are banishing spells more powerful at the dark of the moon.

Full Moon Esbat (Male and female working together)

Couples who may want to work in a circle together should first gather everything that is required in preparation (see page 45–47). When everything is ready the High Priestess (P/ess) and High Priest (P) stand at the edge of where the circle is about to be cast.

The P waits at the east edge of the space to be used while the P/ess moves to the centre of the space and spends a few moments focusing on her intentions. She may raise her hands over her head or clasp her hands in a prayer position, whatever she chooses. When she is ready she says:

I cast this circle with love and light.
Let none be here but in perfect love and perfect truth.

Using the point of her athame, wand, sword, or finger the P/ess walks round the edge, drawing a circle line from the east to the north leaving an open gap with for the P to enter. She approaches the P offering her hand and they say to each other:

P/ess: You who stand on the edge of this magickal space do you wish to enter?
P: I do.
P/ess: And what is in your heart?
P: My heart is filled with perfect truth and perfect love.

The P/ess takes the P's hand, kisses him on the lips, and draws him into the circle. The P stands to one side and the P/ess closes the open gap. The P/ess Lights the alter candle and announces:

Let this circle be illuminated and charged.

The P takes the bell and rings it three times.
The P/ess lights the incense cone, stick, or censer and says:

Let the scent of this incense breathe life and power into this circle.

She hands the incense to the P and he moves to the east and begins to walk slowly round the circle as the P/ess continues to speak saying:

The east, the south, the west and the north.

The P returns the incense to the altar and the P/ess lights a taper from the altar candle and moves from the centre of the circle to the east and lights the east candle and says:

Let the flame from this candle illuminate the east...

She moves slowly round the circle and says:

...the south, the west and the north.

The P/ess and P move to the altar and the P/ess places her finger in the dish of water and focuses her energy into it and says:

I charge thee water of life to purify and consecrate this circle.
She hands the dish of water to the P who moves to the East and begins to sprinkle water slowly round the perimeter saying:

May this sacred water purify, cleanse and give life to the east, the south, the west and the north.

The P/ess and P move to the altar and the P/ess places her finger in the dish of salt and focuses her energy into it. Moving to the east she begins to sprinkle salt around the perimeter saying:

I charge thee salt of life to purify and consecrate the east, the south, the west and the north.

The P rings the bell three times.

The P/ess move to the East and in a powerful voice calls the guardians of the east saying:

Hail to the guardians of the east we bid you come, stand with us, and watch over our circle.

The P moves to the West and in a powerful voice calls the guardians of the west saying:

Hail to the guardians of the west we bid you come, stand with us, and watch over our circle.

The P/ess moves to the south and in a powerful voice calls the guardians of the south saying:

Hail to the guardians of the south we bid you come, stand with us, and watch over our circle.

The P moves to the north and in a powerful voice calls the guardians of the north saying:

Hail to the guardians of the north we bid you come, stand with us, and watch over our circle.

The P returns to the altar whilst the P/ess picks up the athame wand or using her finger and starting at the east moving to the north she draws a pentacle in the air. In the centre of the circle she draws a pentacle over her head and another beneath her feet.

The P joins her in the centre of the circle they hold hands and raise their arms high in the air and silently and reverently focus on the Lord and Lady.

The P speaks saying:

Luna, Lady, high above
We honour and adore you
And give to you our love.
Names you have but many
But no matter which we use
You are the one we worship,
You are the one we choose.

The P/ess says:

Gracious Lord above us
Join us here this night
With your lady by your side
Bless us with your might.
Hear us, show us how to live
To grow and be the best.
Show us how to love and give
Until it's time to rest.

After a few moments they lower their arms but keep their hands joined and the P/ess says:

I am here with you this night
To keep you safe and warm.
I am here when e'er you need
To keep you free from harm.
Worship me in all my forms
As maiden, mother or crone.
Come to me and ask for aid
Whenever you have need.
Be true to me and you will see
Your prayers I will heed.

The P says:

I am here I stand in strength

To watch over you and protect
In kindness truth and love
In honour and respect
I am here beside my Lady
Who is as one with me
Show her your love
Show her your faith
And this you do to me.

Spend some time in quiet meditation or contemplation then you can perform any other magickal workings such as candle or knot magick.

Once the work is done the P says:

We thank the Lord and Lady for being with us tonight. We are grateful for all the gifts that have been given to us and we are open and ready to receive those that are waiting to come to us.

The P/ess says:

The world is an abundant place full of the gifts given to us by mother earth. We accept these gifts with gratitude and will do our best to help those who are less fortunate that we are. We know that whatever is done, it must harm no one for whatever is sent forth will return thrice over.

The P/ess returns to the centre of the altar and rings the bell three times. She pours wine, water or a soft drink into the chalice or cup and raises it above her head
    The Priest raises the athame and places the point into the wine saying:

In this fashion may male and female be joined. Let the fruits of union give life to the work that has been done here tonight.

    This act symbolises the fertilisation of the seed with the earth and the fruition of any magickal work.
The Priest and priestess drink from the chalice or cup and share any food that has been prepared.

The P/ess says:

Eat drink and be merry, share and give thanks.
So mote it be.

When everything is completed the P says:

We have met in love and friendship let us part the same way.
Merry did we meet, merry do we part, merry do we meet again.

The P moves to the east and says:

Take for your use, oh eastern watchtower, any powers of air that have not been used.

The P/ess says:

Take for your use, oh southern watchtower, any powers of fire that have not been used.

The P says:

Take for your use, oh western watchtower, any powers of water that have not been used.

The Priestess says:

Take for your use, oh northern watchtower, any powers of earth that have not been used.

Together they both say:

So mote it be.

They kiss.

Solitary Esbat

The previous ritual could easily be adapted for a solitary. Prepare your altar, cleanse yourself and your space and cast a circle in your usual way and invoke the Goddess. State your intent for this ritual and if it is a full moon Draw Down the Moon.

After this you can perform any spell work or meditate (page 159), pray, prepare and bless your magickal tools and accessories.

Thank the Deity, release the quarters, extinguish the candles and close your circle.

Begin by saying:

I cast this circle with love and light.
Let none be here but in perfect love and perfect truth.

Using the point of the athame, wand, sword, or finger walk round the edge, drawing a circle line from the east to the north:

Light the altar candle and say:

Let this circle be illuminated and charged.

Lights the incense cone, stick, or censer and say:

Let the scent of this incense breathe life and power into this circle.

Move to the east and begin to walk slowly round the circle saying:

The east, the south, the west and the north.

Return the incense to the altar and light a taper from the altar candle and move from the centre of the circle to the east and light the east candle saying:

Let the flame from this candle illuminate the east, the south, the west and the north.

Place your finger in the dish of water and focus your energy into it saying:

I charge thee water of life to purify and consecrate this circle.

Move to the east and sprinkle water slowly round the perimeter saying:

May this sacred water purify, cleanse and give life to the east, the south, the west and the north.

Places your finger in the dish of salt and focus your energy into it. Moving to the east, begin to sprinkle salt around the perimeter saying:

I charge thee salt of life to purify and consecrate the east, the south, the west and the north.

Rings the bell three times. Move to the East and say:

Hail to the guardians of the east I bid you come, stand with me, and watch over this circle.

Moves to the west and say:

Hail to the guardians of the west I bid you come, stand with me, and watch over this circle.

Moves to the south and say:

Hail to the guardians of the south we bid you come, stand with us, and watch over our circle.

Move to the north and say:

Hail to the guardians of the north we bid you come, stand with us, and watch over our circle.

Return to the altar. Pick up the athame, wand or use your finger and starting at the east moving to the north draw a pentacle in the air. In the centre of the circle draws a pentacle over your head and another beneath your feet.

Raise your arms high in the air and silently and reverently focus on the Lord and Lady.

Spend some time in quiet meditation or contemplation then you can perform any other magickal workings such as candle or knot magick.

Once the work is done say:

Thank you Lord and Lady for being with me tonight. I am grateful for your gifts and I am open and ready to receive those that are waiting to come to me.

The world is an abundant place full of the gifts given to us by mother earth. I accept these gifts with gratitude and will do my best to help those who are less fortunate that I am. I know that whatever is done, it must harm no one for whatever is sent forth will return thrice over.

Return to the centre of the altar and ring the bell three times. Pour wine, water or a soft drink into the chalice or cup and raise it above your head

Drink from the chalice or cup and eat any food that has been prepared.

Eat drink and be merry, and give thanks.
So mote it be.

Moves to the east and say:

Take for your use, oh eastern watchtower, any powers of air that have not been used.

Take for your use, oh southern watchtower, any powers of fire that have not been used.

Take for your use, oh western watchtower, any powers of water that have not been used.

Take for your use, oh northern watchtower, any powers of earth that have not been used.

So mote it be.

Handfasting Ceremony

Beltane is the best time for handfasting. The circle should be cast before the guests arrive and a doorway should be left open to allow the guests to enter.

The best man/priest should stand to the right of the opening and the best maid/priestess should stand to the left of the opening. As the guests queue to enter, the best man/priest should take the first lady's hand and say:

In what manner do you enter this circle?

She should reply:

In perfect truth and perfect love.

The best man/priest should 'pull' her into the circle and she should walk all the way round the circle in a clockwise direction till she reaches the best man/priest. The best maid/priestess should take the first man's hand and say:

In what manner do you enter this circle?

He should reply:

In perfect truth and perfect love.

The best maid/priestess should 'pull' him into the circle and he should walk all the way round the circle in a clockwise direction till he reaches the first lady.

This process should be repeated until all the guests are assembled at which point the best man/priest and the best maid/priestess should leave the circle to fetch the bride and groom. The best maid/priestess brings the groom into the circle and walks round the circle clockwise then back to the altar and places him to the right of the altar. The best man/priest brings the bride into the circle and walks round the circle clockwise then back to the altar and places her to the left of the altar.

The high priestess raises her arms to the sky and says:

We gather in this sacred place
And stand together face to face.
Our promises we make today
Never broken come what may.

The groom says:

Without you my days are dark and empty and my nights are long and cold.

The bride says:

Without you I have no purpose, no future to unfold.

The groom says:

Join me, make my life complete.

The bride says:

With you my life's replete.

The groom says:

I [insert groom's name] *promise to love, cherish and adore you from this day forth.*

The bride says:

I [insert bride's name] *promise to love, cherish and adore you from this day forth.*

The high priestess holds a censer of incense high in front of the bride and groom and asks:

In what manner do you make this promise?

Facing the east, the bride and groom say:

By the air that we breathe we make this promise.

The high priestess replaces the censer of incense and raises a candle high in front of the bride and groom and says:

In what manner do you make this promise?

Facing the south, the bride and groom say:

By the fire in our loins we make this promise.

The high priestess replaces the candle and sprinkles the bride and groom with consecrated water and asks:

In what manner do you make this promise?

Facing the west, the bride and groom say:

By the water that gives us life, we make this promise.

The high priestess replaces the consecrated water and holds a dish of soil in front of the bride and groom and asks:

In what manner do you make this promise?

Facing the north, the bride and groom say:

By the earth that holds our weight we make this promise.

The high priestess hands a chalice of wine to the bride and an athame to the groom and they turn and face each other. The high priestess holds her hands up high and invokes the God and the Goddess while the best man/priest and best maid/priestess take the wedding rings and drop them into the wine. The high priestess says:

May the Lord and Lady and all here present witness this rite and may [insert bride's name] *and* [insert the groom's name] *be joined together.*

May the Lord and Lady bless this union so that it be fruitful and filled with love.

As the high priestess says these words the groom should place the athame into the wine and remain in that position until the high priestess is ready. In this fashion may man and woman be joined. The high priestess asks:

Where are the rings?

The groom uses the point of the athame to remove the rings from the chalice. The best maid/priestess steps forward with the consecrated water and the high priestess rinses the bride's ring in the water and offers it to the groom who places it on the bride's finger. The high priestess rinses the groom's ring in the water and offers it to the bride who places it on the groom's finger. The best man/priest then steps forward with a white cord or ribbon and the high priestess wraps the cords in a figure of eight round the bride and groom's wrists and ties them. She says:

As these rings represent the circle that binds your love so too do these cords represent the circle that binds your lives together.
By the power and the blessings of the Lord and Lady you are now joined as husband and wife.
The bride and groom kiss.

The best man/priest and best maid/priestess lay a broomstick on the ground and the bride and the groom jump the broomstick.

Naming Ceremony

I prepared this circle for one of my readers and it was performed by the grandmother. If you have a family member who would like to carry out the naming ceremony for your child please feel free to adapt the following to suit your needs. You should have the usual circle requirements as well as blessing cards for each of your guests so that they can write down their blessings for your baby. Gifts should be non-tangible, such as health, beauty, skills, and such like.

The circle should be cast in your usual fashion and an inner circle should be cast for the high priestess/grandmother, the parents, godparents and baby. The guests should remain in the outer circle (or semicircle if your garden is small). A doorway should be left open in the inner circle with an archway if possible.

The parents and godparents should be standing to the edges of the inner circle with females to the left and males to the right.

If there are two sets of grandparents they can of course both be involved in the ceremony.

The grandmother calls upon the Lord and Lady to witness the blessing and when she is ready she invites the mother and father (without the baby) into the circle. She places her hands on the top of their heads and blesses the mother and father in her own words. This done the mother stands to her left and the father to her right. The grandmother calls:

Who stands for this child?

The godparent or godparents answer:

I/we do.

The grandmother welcomes them with the baby into the circle. The godfather holds the baby while the grandmother places her hand on the godmother's head and blesses her. The godmother then holds the baby while the godfather receives a similar blessing.

The grandmother takes the baby from the godmother and holds it high and presents the child to the Lord and Lady and blesses the child with gifts of health and happiness (or whatever she wishes) finishing with:

I name this child [insert the baby's name], *may she/he live a long and healthy life filled with joy.*

This done, she carries the baby to the first guest and places the baby in the guest's arms. They hold the baby and looking into the baby's eyes bless the baby saying:

I bless [the baby's name] *with the gift of* [insert gift].

This done, they then pass the baby to the next guest who does the same. The baby is passed round all the guests and finally given back to the grandmother who passes the baby to the mother. The grandmother thanks the Lord and Lady for witnessing the blessing and closes the circle.

Sabbats

In the Wiccan or Pagan Wheel of the Year there are eight Sabbats. Four of these Sabbats are know as Greater Sabbats and four are Lesser Sabbats. The four Lesser Sabbats are the Spring and Autumn Equinoxes, and the Summer and Winter Solstices.

Imbolc = Greater Sabbat = 2nd February

Imbolc is also known as Candlemas or the Festival of Lights because of the tradition of lighting candles throughout the house. This festival is dedicated to the Goddess Brigid who is the Goddess of blacksmiths, creativity, healing, wisdom, fertility, and childbirth.

At Imbolc we know that spring is about to happen and the earth begins to awaken. This is a perfect time to spring clean the house from top to bottom, open all the windows, and let out the stale winter air and welcomes the fresh and new into your home.

When your house has been cleaned from top to bottom light some candles in celebration of the arrival of spring and the rebirth of the Sun. It's not just about cleaning the house though, detox your mind, body and spirit. Clear you mind of all negative thoughts and begin to plan for the year ahead. Think about old patterns or habits that you have and want to change as this is the perfect time to make these changes.

Start an exercise or diet programme and get your body in good working order. Make a list of any foods/habits that you could do without and cut them out of your diet or shopping list, then make a list of all the foods that will be good for you.

Spend some time meditating using crystals, a candle flame, or the sound of relaxing music and replenish your spirit energy too.

Make a point of planning some 'Me Time' into your new schedule.

Once you have cleaned the house and made changes to improve your life and lifestyle you could think about performing rituals such as a Self Dedication rite (page 58). Traditionally Imbolc is the best time to do this but of course it can be done at other times. You can perform just about any ritual you like any time you like but some will work better than others at given times for example since Brigid is the Goddess of creativity, healing, wisdom, fertility, and childbirth then this would be a good time to perform rituals for any of these purposes.

Soon we will begin to plant seeds for our garden or allotment and it is possible to grow salad vegetables in window boxes or pots on window sills.

We should prepare our seeds by performing a simple ceremony to bless them before planting them in the coming months.

Imbolc Chakra Opening Meditation

Choose a time and place where you are unlikely to be disturbed, lock the door, take the phone off the hook, find a comfortable and safe space where you will not be disturbed.

Close your eyes and relax and take deep breaths in, and as you do so visualise that you are breathing in positive light energy. As you breathe out let all the dark negative energy go. Feel that all the stress and discomfort and difficulties of the past few days or weeks or months are being expelled on the out breaths. Again relax and when you feel that you are ready.

Visualise a beam of light above your head. See this light which is connected to infinity above coming down and resting on your crown Chakra. As it touches the Lotus bud on your crown the bud begins to open into a beautiful flower. Let the light rest there for a moment.

Let the light move to your Third Eye where it finds the bud of a beautiful Orchid. As the light touches the Orchid it begins to blossom and open. Let the light rest there for a moment.

Let it move to your Throat Chakra where it finds the bud of a beautiful Bluebell. As the light touches the Bluebell it begins to blossom and open. Let the light rest there for a moment.

Let it move to your Heart Chakra where it finds the bud of a beautiful Rose. As the light touches the Rose it begins to blossom and open. Let the light rest there for a moment.

Let it move to your Solar Plexus Chakra where it finds the bud of a beautiful Sunflower. As the light touches the Sunflower it begins to blossom and open. Let the light rest there for a moment.

Let it move to your Sacral Chakra where it finds the bud of a beautiful Poppy. As the light touches the Poppy it begins to blossom and open. Let the light rest there for a moment.

Let it move to your Base Chakra where it finds the sapling of a beautiful Oak Tree. As the light touches the sapling it begins to open and grow. The roots of the sapling begin to travel downwards towards the centre of infinity below. Stronger and larger the roots of the oak tree grow moving further down through your legs and feet until finally they are firmly connected to the source of infinity below you. Let the light rest there for a moment and then begin to draw healing energy from the core centre of the earth beneath you into your body through these roots.

Draw the healing energy up to your base Chakra and allow it to merge with the light energy from the source of infinity above you. Allow the energy from above and below to circulate throughout your entire being healing purifying and repairing anything that is required. See all your Chakras open and functioning fully. When you are ready to finish visualise your Guardian Angel spreading a protective cloak on your shoulders and enveloping your entire being in this cloak of protection. Gradually allow yourself to come back into reality, stretch, take a deep breath and open your eyes. Always rise slowly after a meditation and eat something to make sure that you are fully grounded and awake.

Imbolc = Self dedication rite
Gather together all the things that you will need

Tall Candles & holders, small tea light candles, matches, salt, water, an athame or wand, small dishes anointing oil that you can make yourself perhaps using frankincense, myrrh and marjoram or another combination of oils if you prefer. It is more important that your mind is focused on your intention and that your intention is honourable and does not interfere with another persons will. Your thoughts must be pure and sincere and your wishes should be for positive reasons rather than negative ones. You must remember that whatever you put out will come back to you threefold. When you have gathered together all the items that you are going to use and you have prepared your self and your surroundings you may move on to the next step.

Follow the self-dedication rite on page 58 or create your own.

Imbolc Blessing Seeds Rite
Gather together all the items that you are going to use including any seeds that you are going to bless and any items from the list of magickal component under the heading 'Fertility' on page 139.

Follow the procedure for casting your circle on page 48 until you reach part 12. Lay all your seeds out and focus your attention on the energy that you have gathered, Now spend a few moments with the palms of your hands moving over the seeds and visualise them being blessed with pure white light energy. If you have been attuned to Reiki and you are familiar with 'the Dragon's Breath' you can use this technique and bless your seeds in this way. Once you have completed your task. Replace the seeds in a suitable container and resume your ceremony from where you left off.

Ostara = Eostar = Lesser Sabbat = March 21st, Spring Equinox

Eostar or Ostara is the first day of spring when both night and day are of equal length. At this time we give back to the earth by planting seeds that were gathered from the last harvest. Of course your seeds may have come from your local garden centre but there is nothing wrong with that. Our seeds which we blessed at Imbolc should be sown now in gardens window boxes or plant pots and we will be keeping this eternal cycle of life going.

During this festival we worship the Goddess Ostara. At this time the Goddess is a young maiden, beautiful in her youth, full of life and vigour, fertile in every way. Stop and think for a moment of young girls around the age of sixteen to nineteen years old. They fuss about their appearance and their figures but when we look at them we just see their beauty. That is the beauty of the Goddess at this time.

The same applies to the earth beneath our feet which is striving to produce new growth and we have a responsibility to tend to that new growth in any way that we can so that it too becomes beautiful to look at.

The egg is the symbol of Ostara or Eostar which is where the Easter egg custom comes from. The egg is the symbol of fertility and life and we should focus of our attention on new beginnings recoveries and rebirths.

You might want to try dying boiled eggs, my mum's favourites for this were tea leaves and beetroot juice, but here are some suggestions for a variety of colours

Colour	Ingredients
Blue	Blueberries
	Red cabbage
Brown	Coffee
	Tea
Green	Spinach
Orange	White onion skins (in quantity)
	Chilli powder
	Paprika
Pink/red	Beetroot
	Cranberries
	Raspberries
	Cherries
Purple	Red onion skins

	Red wine
	Garden huckleberries (a very vivid purple)
Yellow	Orange peel
	Lemon peel
	Carrots
	White onion skins
	Cumin
	Turmeric

You can boil the eggs in any of the above ingredients added to water but there is another way which makes really pretty eggs if you are having an Ostara Ritual Celebration with plenty of people to feed.

Boil your eggs in the normal way without adding any colour then strain them and lay them on a dry tea towel. Carefully crack the shells all over so that the shells are cracked all the way through to the egg but the egg is still covered and the shells are still in place. Set up a few pots with your coloured liquids and put the cracked boiled eggs into the coloured liquids and boil again. Later when you remove the shells you will have beautifully decorated boiled eggs. They are so pretty and look wonderful on a salad platter. You will have to have one extra to test the colour density but it's worth the effort.

Think of family too at this Sabbat, particularly your mother or grandmother, and spend time with them if you can. If you are not fortunate enough to be able to do that perhaps you can take some spring flowers and decorated eggs to an elderly friend or neighbour and make this time special for them too.

If you are very brave and artistic you can try blowing eggs and painting the shells for an everlasting reminder but that requires more effort and finesse. To do this you have to pierce the egg shell at both ends and blow the contents out through the little holes. Squeeze or blow too hard and you will end up with a real mess but if you can do this you can make really beautiful mementoes.

Decorate your house with spring flowers such as daffodils and narcissi and a platter of boiled coloured eggs for any Easter visitors and leave an offering plate outside with some seeds for wild birds and of course the fairies.

Ostara ritual to banish negativity

Gather together all the items that you are going to use including:

- Some blessed seeds (sunflower seeds are perfect for this)
- A plant pot
- A container with enough of soil to fill the plant pot
- A sheet of paper
- A pen
- A small jug of water to water the seeds after you have planted them

See instructions for banishing rituals on pages 25, 26, 28, 109, 122 and 190. Banishing rituals take place during a waning moon.

Follow the procedure for casting your circle on page 48 until you reach part 12. Sit quietly in your sacred space and think of the past year and any problems that have affected your life. As you think of each problem, write it down. When you have completed your list, half fill the plant pot with soil then lay the piece of paper on top of the soil. Next fill the pot to almost the top and lay your blessed seeds on the soil. Cover the seeds with a fine layer of soil and carefully water. As you perform this rite say a few words of your own choosing, or use these words:

Problems in the past I had
And many did I know
But now I bury all the bad
And ask these seeds to grow
And as they grow they feed upon
That I no longer want
My problems now they will be gone
As my seed becomes a plant
Grow for me and flower too
My problems now are gone
This coming year will be so good
As problems I have none
An it harm none so mote it be.

Now spend a few moments and cup your hands round your plant pot and visualise them being blessed with pure white light energy. If you have been attuned to Reiki you can use 'the Dragon's Breath' technique again.

Once you have completed your task resume your ceremony from where you left off.

Ostara property ritual
Selling a house

Cast your circle in the normal way and when you are ready cut out the picture of the house you are selling as it appears on your schedule.

Write across it in bold print SOLD FOR £***** (insert the price that you hope to achieve) and put the date of the spell under the selling price.

Put it into a frame with a silver or gold coin and an old key

Sit the framed picture somewhere prominent and light a tea light candle in front of it and burn this candle continuously (if possible). When the candle burns out, light another. Each time you look at the picture say a little prayer to your God. If you have to put the candle out DO NOT BLOW IT OUT wet your fingers and pinch it out or use a candle snuff.

Renting a house

Trying to move to a new rented property - follow these instructions Cut out a picture showing the area and type of home you want to move to.

Write across it in bold print MY NEW HOME £***** per month (insert the rental figure that you can afford) and put the date of the spell under the rental figure.

Put it into a frame with a silver or gold coin and an old key

Sit the framed picture somewhere prominent and light a candle in front of it and burn this candle continuously (if possible). When the candle burns out, light another. Each time you look at the picture say a little prayer to your God.

Ostara ritual to invoke prosperity

The above ritual can be used with an invoking verse for any purpose or you can use the one below.

Follow the procedure for casting your circle on page 48 until you reach part 12. Lay out everything that you require including

- a piece of citrine (The merchants' crystal)
- a dish full of coins with some red ribbon loosely laid on top of them
- use a gold and silver candle on the altar
- dress the altar with a gold or silver cloth if you can
- use the following Tarot Cards, King, Ten and Four Pentacles and any other items that you may wish to use from the list of magickal component under the heading of prosperity

Lord and Lady here me call, welcome to this place
I ask of you this special day, to look upon my face
Bless me with your love and care and keep me safe from harm
Bless me with abundance and keep me well and warm
Thanks to you I am fulfilled of that I can be sure
My love for you forever will be both true and pure
An it harm none so mote it be

Once you have completed your task resume your ceremony from where you left off.

Beltane = Greater Sabbat = April 30th.

This is a very special and joyous time for followers of the old ways. We celebrate the emergence of the Goddess as the May Queen and the God as the May King. This is a time of sensuality and sexuality. The Maypole represents the phallus to show rampant virility. The burying of the Maypole, the phallus, in the earth, Mother Earth is symbolic of their union.

If you think about the May Queen, the Goddess, as being Mother Earth and the May King, the God being the Sun when the join in harmony the earth begins to swell with growth and new life just as the maiden does when she marries, handfasts her beloved and their union produces a child.

This too, as at Ostara is a time of fertility, but with a heightened sensuality.

Seeds that have been sown should be sprouting now and this applies to not just actual seeds for plants but for the seeds of ideas and plans that began earlier. In the traditions of the old ways couples declare their love and commitment to each other by being handfasted for a year and a day, for life, or for eternity.

Bonfires are lit all over the land and celebrations and parades are held and people dance round the Maypole. New unions are formed between couples who may even become handfasted at the next Beltane festival.

To celebrate Beltane rise just before the dawn and as the Sun rises wash your face in the early morning dew. This is said to bring good fortune and bless you with health and beauty. Sing and dance if possible and enjoy this special time. Prepare a May basket by filling it with flowers and include some Rowan twigs for good luck then give it to someone.

If you live near the sea, a river or stream or have a pond of your own, scatter some flower heads on the water and give thanks to the element of water for giving sustenance to the land.

Beltane Handfasting Ceremony

A handfasting ceremony is a very beautiful and special time for the bride and groom just as in any other marriage ceremony and just as much care and attention to detail goes into the preparation. When my husband and I married we had a registry office wedding and then went home and had a handfasting in our garden with about thirty close friends and family members. The fact that I was a Solitary made this a little more complicated to arrange and I must admit that I was a little apprehensive about any reaction from everyone but in reality I had nothing at all to worry about and everyone loved the occasion.

I prepared my circle prior to the registry office ceremony and when the time was right we asked our guest to form a circle. My bridesmaid Margaret acted as a narrator following a script that I had prepared earlier and I stepped up to my circle and stood at the edge invoking the Goddess. I had already filled both hands with sparkling confetti and my hands were in the Goddess position crossed in front of my chest. There was a total silence behind me and as I stepped into my circle I spread my hands raising them high above me and let go of the sparkling confetti which cascaded all around me. There was an audible gasp and I heard my son Ian say 'My mother is pure magick'. A little touch of the dramatic coupled with a little humour and the ice was broken. From that point forward everything went beautifully. I welcomed Martin into my space in perfect truth and perfect love, we exchanged our solemn vows with each other, and Margaret stepped forward and tied our hands together with white cords. Margaret pronounced us duly handfasted and invited us to 'Jump the Broomstick'. Of course with much hilarity everyone had to have a turn of jumping the broomstick too. Some consider jumping the broomstick as a wish for fertility in the coming year, I wonder would so many have jumped it had they known.

I keep my cords in a silver filigree box along with the cork from the champagne bottle that was splashed all over us (a spirit blessing). My box sits on a display shelf in our lounge. A silver Dragon holding a gem encrusted moon sits on the top of the box and our wedding picture sits beside that. I still smile every time I look over and see them and I remember that special day.

If you wish to be handfasted you can you can request the services of an official celebrant to perform one for you or create a simple ceremony yourself.

Beltane Wiccaning Ceremony

What made our handfasting extra special was that after the handfasting I carried out a wiccaning, naming or blessing ceremony for my granddaughter Eva. This is like a Christening or Baptism in Christian services but the differences are that everyone gets the chance to hold the baby and give a special gift. The gifts though are not tangible gifts, like clothes or soft toys, they are blessings.

Our circle was still in place and I called the parents into the circle in perfect truth and perfect love. I gave a Goddess blessing to my daughter and her partner and baby Eva and then Eva was handed round the circle with each person holding her for a few minutes, looking into her eyes and saying there blessing out loud. Eva was about four months old at the time and big enough to enjoy the whole procedure. She was just a perfect participant gazing at everyone as they blessed her. She received so many beautiful gifts; the gift of music, the gift of love, the gift of laughter, the gift of honesty. One of our good friends Tom who is a Royal Marine gave her 'A sense of adventure, a nose for trouble, and the ability to get her self out of it' quite appropriate for his life style and she does have that sort of dynamic spirit twinkling in her beautiful eyes. My Granddaughter Ashia was about five years old at the time and she too held Eve and gave her the gift of 'Lots of toys'.

The whole procedure was a wonderful experience for everyone and I have never seen so many grown men cry.

Again you can have an official celebrant do this for you or you can arrange something quite simple yourself. Make a list of blessings so that if your non-pagan or non-wiccan guests aren't sure what to bless the baby with, they have something to stimulate their ideas.

Litha = Lesser Sabbat = June 22nd = Summer Solstice

On this special day the Goddess is at the height of Her power, impregnated at Beltane She is now pregnant with the God whom she will give birth to once more at the Winter Solstice. This is a time for like minds to gather and share the bounty of some of the herbs that have been grown. The trees in full bloom are now abundant with twigs that can be cut and made into wands. This must be done respectfully by mentally or verbally blessing the tree and asking for permission to use the selected branch. I would generally leave a small crystal or some token at the base of the tree as a gift. Lovers continue to be handfasted during this time and everyone enjoys the abundance that Mother Earth provides us with.

We remember too the battle between Oak King, God of the waxing year and Holly King, God of the waning year. Some covens will enact this but as a Solitary it is enough to remember that the Wheel of the Year continues to turn and that which was born must live and die before being reborn again and again just as the plants of the earth do.

A Witch's Ladder should be made which can be used time and time again to empower magickal rituals. To make, use three lengths of ribbon each of a different colour. You can use red, black, and white for the Triple Goddess or perhaps choose other colours to suit your preference. Pleat the ribbons together until they are three feet long. These Witches Ladders make a lovely tree decoration if you are fortunate enough to have trees nearby or in your garden. You can add shells or charms to them as you choose. For magickal workings you can add tokens, charms or anything that is suitable to your spell such as keys for property spells, coins for money spells, crystals that have been dedicated for specific purposes; the choice is endless, experiment and enjoy the process rather than worrying if you are doing it right. Your intention is more important than the accuracy of your performance.

You can also make a Solar Wheel and hang it in your house or on a tree or bush in your garden for the God's protection. For best results use willow or vine and wind it into a circle about the size of a dinner plate. Secure the ends using a natural twine and then cut two short lengths of stem longer than the diameter of the circle. Place one across the centre horizontally and the other one across the centre vertically and secure them in place. These too can be decorated with charms ribbons or pouches containing magickal powders.

Litha is longest day of the year and the shortest night so you will have plenty of time to do all the things that you want to do especially divination and ritualistic magick. If you do not already have a scrying mirror or a scrying globe you could add this to you 'things to do list' and make them yourself following the instructions below.

To make a Scrying Mirror

You will need:
- a glass picture frame (I bought mine for fifteen pounds in a second had shop it has and oval antique brass filigree frame on a swivel holder). Make sure that it is glass and not Perspex.
- black gloss paint
- paint brush
- newspaper to lay your work on

Lay out your sheets of newspaper then take the glass out of the frame and apply several coats of black gloss paint to the glass. Allow plenty of time between coats to be sure that the paint is dry. Once the paint is dry reassemble the glass and the frame and then bless or consecrate your scrying mirror during a Full Moon Esbat.

Keep your scrying mirror covered with a black silk cloth or scarf except when the moon is full. When the moon is full allow your mirror to stand uncovered facing the moon and absorbing the energy. Do not let anyone but you look into or handle your scrying mirror.

To Make a Scrying Globe

Most towns have a shop selling lamps, lamp shades and various electrical fittings. What you need to look for is a small round glass shade, the kind you would put on a ceiling light or stand on a small surface. Some of these come in frosted or cloudy glass but you will want a completely clear glass globe. I have seen them in a few stores but they are not always clear. If you are searching the Internet for a supplier near you, you should use 'clear glass globe shade' as your search sentence.

They are not easy to find, if you are meant to have one it will appear when the time is right. Once you have found one though follow these instructions for making your scrying globe.

Gather together:
- your glass globe (not Perspex).
- black gloss paint
- newspaper to lay your work on
- a mixing bowl slightly bigger than your globe.

Lay out your sheets of newspaper then dismantle the globe from any base that it may be attached to (they sometimes come on wooden bases).

Turn it upside down with the opening to the top and very carefully pour a little of the black gloss paint into the globe and begin to turn it round and round until you have completely coated the globe. If you have not poured in enough paint add more and if you have used too much pour it back into the paint tin. Once you have completely covered the glass sit the bowl with the opening to the top in the baking dish. Check this every few minutes and if excess paint has gathered in the bottom just lift it out carefully and pour it into your paint tin. Do this several times allowing plenty of time between coats to be sure that each layer has dried completely. Once the paint is dry replace the base to the globe and then bless, or consecrate your scrying globe during a Full Moon Esbat.

Keep your scrying globe covered with a black silk cloth or scarf except when the moon is full. When the moon is full allow your globe to stand uncovered where the moon can bless it with its energy and recover it with its scarf or cloth and store as usual in a sacred or private place. Do not let anyone but you look into or handle your scrying globe.

Litha Scrying/Divination Ritual

This ritual can be used to ask for guidance in divination skills. Follow the procedure for casting your circle on page 48 until you reach part 12.

Lay out everything that you require including :

- a deck of Tarot Cards spread so that you can see the images with the High Priest or Hierophant uppermost.
- A crystal ball scrying globe or scrying mirror (if you have one)
- rune stones or cards
- dice
- a teacup that you have drunk from with tea leaves still at the bottom and any items of your choice from the 'Divination and Prophesy' list of magickal components (page 138).

Once you have invoked the Goddess and you begin your magickal work use a verse of your own choice or repeat this verse and as you do so, hand the cards, runes or any of the divination objects on your altar. Repeat the wishes part over and over again until it becomes a chant.

Lady and Lord this day is long
As night approaches I worship thee
I work and play and sing my song
I sing my song my prayer to thee

I ask of you to grant to me
Wishes one and two and three
My worship is both true and pure
My thanks I offer to be sure

Let me see what lies ahead. To be hopeful, never dread
Let me see the mystery. Understanding grant to me
Let me know the truth unfold
My words then doth Wisdom hold
Repeat

Finish your ritual by using any of your divination tools and record anything that you have seen then close your circle in the usual way.

Lammas = Greater Sabbat = July 31st

Lammas, also known as Lughnasadh, is named for the God Lugh. The Goddess as Mother Earth is worshipped for the rich bounty that she has bestowed us with. The Sun God weakens at this stage and is slowly dying as the days grow shorter and we move towards winter. The Goddess knows that the God is dying, but lives on inside Her as Her child.

Herbs roots and flower petals that we have sown should be ready to harvest and these can be spread, hung and dried and stored in airtight containers or if appropriate chopped and frozen. The first batch of jams and flower syrups can be made and these too can be stored for future use.

The main symbols at this celebration are corns and grains. We can make corn dollies to decorate our altar or house and we celebrate the first harvest.

If you can obtain a bunch of wheat you can make a Corn Dolly. Fold the sheaves of wheat in half and keep the fronds to the top as the head. Tie this tight at the waist and neck and then take a shorter bunch and tie them across where the arms would be. You can be as creative as you like adding small pieces of fabric as a dress and perhaps even making a small hat or scarf.

Witch's Bottle

This is a good time to make a Witch's Bottle to protect us from negative energies or any harm that may come our way during the winter months to follow.

Use a lidded glass jar and decorate it with bright colours. Paint the runic symbol Eohl on the front and back of the jar then fill it with old needles, pins, nails or screws, and any broken glass or pottery. Bury this near the doorway of your home or in a large plant pot sat outside your front door to keep harm away from you and yours. This can be done before or after your Lammas ritual.

Witch's Ladder

You could also attempt a Witch's Ladder made from corn and tie coloured pouches of magickal powders at various intervals along its length and hang it near the front door inside your house. Each time you leave or enter the house you can touch the magickal pouches to empower your intentions.

Lammas Ritual for Protection

You can perform a ritual to honour the Lord and Lady as well as gratitude and protection rituals at this time or indeed any ritual of your own choice.

For a protection ritual, cast your circle as normal and include all the items that you will need to make a Witches Bottle you can include in it herbs or spices from the list of magickal components under the heading protection and you can have various items on your altar from the same listing. Prepare your Witches Bottle in circle and as you do so chant the following verses

Little bottle full of pins
Sharp and jagged edges
Keep away the one who sins
Away from all our hedges

Keep us safe and keep us warm
Watch o'er us when we're sleeping
Keep us safe and free from harm
And always in your keeping

When you are finished close your circle in the usual way and take your little bottle to your chosen place and bury it near your gate or door. If you don't have a garden you could use a large plant pot or flower box at your door.

Mabon = Lesser Sabbat = September 21st = Autumn Equinox

Night and day are equal in length on this the first day of thanksgiving and gratitude should be the focus of our intentions. Our rituals should be to give thanks for the harvest that we reap form Mother Earth. We make preparation for the winter by storing fruits and fruit pies and jams. We should also think about those other gifts that we have received. At Imbolc we sowed the seeds of new plans and ideas and now is the time to look back and review where we started and the progress that we have made with these plans.

The God continues his descent into the underworld and soon winter will be upon us and the night will grow longer and the days will grow shorter; we too will descend into the darkness of the winter. The season of Mother Earth's Fertility is growing to a close and she too will descend into the underworld soon to await the coming year and the start of a new cycle.

Mabon Ritual for Gratitude/Protection

Now is the time to give thanks for the summer blessings that we have received but we should also think about the coming months and the way the weather will change and the effects that this will have on the land the frail the elderly and sometimes the young too. We are blessed indeed in this modern society that we don't have to go out in the cold and the wet to the outside barn to collect from our stores and we are blessed too with plentiful supplies of foods and medicines all year round. But don't be fooled by that because there are still those among us who have little. There are still those among us who are sick or elderly and in poor health and we should spare a thought and perform a kind deed or give to a charity in gratitude that we are better off than they because no matter how bad you may think things are there is always someone who is worse off than you.

Think of these things whilst you celebrate this Mabon and perform a suitable ritual of your choice or use the one below.

Cast your circle in the usual way and decorate your altar with the appropriate colours herbs spices or flowers and any items from the list of magickal components under the heading of Gratitude and/or Protection on pages 142 and 150. You can use the verse below or another of your choice to suit your ritual.

Thanks we give for all received
From seeds that we have sown
We watched our crops in fields of green
And we're blessed with what we've grown

Soon winter comes and we grow cold
Though fires burning brightly
We tend the frail we tend the old
We keep our vigil nightly

We here do ask our stocks and stores
Our flour for bread our harvest too
May keep again till springtime comes
And last the winter through

When you have finished close your circle in the normal fashion.

Samhain = Greater Sabbat = October 31st.

Samhain commonly known as Halloween is a really special time in the Wheel of the Year. The 'veil' between the spiritual world and the earth is at its thinnest and we can connect easier with those loved ones or wise ones who have gone before us and they can connect with us. Because of the nature of this festival of Samhain it is sometimes referred to as All Souls ' Day. We celebrate the lives of our loved ones who have passed over and carry out a ritual of remembrance. This is a good time to meditate on these loved ones and tell them things that we didn't get the chance to say or ask them for advice. In some customs it is common for covens or families to lay a place at the table for a loved one who has passed over.

The God completes his descent into the underworld and the earth begins to rest and grow still for the winter months. The Goddess heavily pregnant goes to rest before the birth of the new God at Yule.

The weather gets colder and everyone begins to wrap up well against the cold. In these winter months many people do not survive the onslaught of colds and flues and germs but this happened more so in times gone by so performing rituals of protection and would be common place.

In practical terms this is the last of the three harvest festivals that began at Lammas and again more preparations of salves and healing aids would be made and stored as would ciders and wines. Seeds form crops would be saved and labelled and stored safely for the new season's plantings and these would be blessed at Imbolc.

You can perform any ritual of your choice or you could try the one shown below to invite communication from any loved one who has passed over or perhaps a guardian angle or spirit guide.

Samhain Ritual for Spirituality

Cast your circle in the usual way but when you are calling up the quarters do so in the following fashion:

Hail to the Guardian of the Watchtower of the East element of Air – Let none do enter except they do so in perfect truth and perfect love.
The veil is lifted the way is clear
Hail to the Guardian of the Watchtower of the South element of Fire – Let none do enter except they do so in perfect truth and perfect love.
Hail to the Guardian of the Watchtower of the West element of water – Let none do enter except they do so in perfect truth and perfect love.
Hail to the Guardian of the Watchtower of the North element of earth – Let none do enter except they do so in perfect truth and perfect love.
When you have invoked the Goddess contemplate on any questions you may have for a departed loved one or any guidance you require and repeat the verse below
Wise Ones, Elders come to me
The open door gives entry
Angels, Loved Ones guide us now
They can pass the guardian sentry
Now's the time that we do bow
To wisdom from above
Teach us that which we should know
That comes with light and love

Yule = Lesser Sabbat = December 21st = Winter Solstice

This is the first day of winter and the day is shorter than the night. This would be a time of celebration having survived the worst of the winter people could look forward to the New Year with renewed hope. In today's society we would make a New Year resolution on the 31st of December. In the old faith this resolution would be made at Yule. As with other faiths we would exchange gifts, sing dance and celebrate with friends and family. In past times people would not be afraid to use up supplies because they would know that spring would arrive soon and the earth would once more be abundant with fish and game and blessings from the soil.

The Goddess gives birth to the new God, the Sun God on this day and we light Yule logs and candles in celebration of this event. Rituals could include magickal workings for friendship, creativity, and success as well as healing for the vulnerable

To carry out a friendship ritual cast your circle in the normal way and lay your altar decorated with traditional seasonal things. You can include any of the items that are listed under 'Friendship' in the magickal components section on page 140. When you have invoked the Goddess repeat this verse or use one of your own choice:

Yule Rituals for Friendship and Success

For friendship

Our friends may come and they may go
But always they will be
Close to my heart and in my thoughts
Wherever they may be

They have no doubts they always know
Our love doth cross o'er land and see
Our friendship travels where they go
And lasts eternally

For Success

Hear my spell I ask of you
My Lady from above
Success to us in all we do
And blessed with light and love

Success may come and it may go
The wheel doth ever turn
But what we do and what we know
Work hard and we will earn

For efforts made rewards we reap
The Lady blesses those
She grant to us, our bounty keep
Her love to us she shows

Create Magickal Energy

There may be times when you need to create a spell instantly and you may not be in a situation where you can cast a circle or draw down the moon. Your hands will be the tool of convenience at time like these. Focus your intention on your purpose then visualise that you are in a protective bubble of light; this is your portable circle. Once you have done this clasp your hands together as though you were washing them. As you do this focus all your energy and intention on your hands and gradually you will feel them becoming warmer. Continue this until you have mentally empowered and visualised your intention and utter the words to convey your desire and as you separate your hands make a gesture as though you were pushing something away and say 'An it harm none so mote it be'.

Using one hand

This is your emergency procedure when you cannot carry out the above exercise because you can do this one with your hand in your pocket. Use your index finger and rotate it in a clockwise direction while you visualise that you are in a protective bubble of light. Mentally empower and visualise your intention and inwardly utter the words to convey your desire then taking your hand from your pocket snap your fingers and release your spell remembering to say 'An it harm none so mote it be'.

Dancing

Covens would generally dance in a clockwise direction during a ritual to empower the energy however this is very difficult if you are a Solitary as you could end up dizzy and on your bottom – not very spiritual – but there is no reason why you cannot just dance for the joy of the occasion whilst focusing your intention and when you are spent you can drop to the floor or a chair and release the energy whilst uttering the words 'An it harm none so mote it be'.

Chanting

There are several faiths or disciplines that practice chanting such as Hindu,

Jewish, Islamic and even Anglican. Probably the most commonly recognised method of chanting is Buddhist Chanting. A practising Buddhist would chant Nam Myoho Renge Kyo, to be aware, to receive enlightenment, and to heal.

As a Reiki Master, I chant the names of the Reiki healing symbols during treatments for clients or to myself to help me to overcome any difficult situation that I may find myself in. On one occasion my husband and I were touring on his motorbike and we had to travel over a very rough road. He stopped and surveyed the road ahead and looked over his shoulder at me.

'Do you trust me?' he said.

'With my life' I replied.

And then he started to move forward carefully negotiating the ruts and rubble. I did and still do trust him but I must admit that I did my Reiki Chant for the rest of the journey until we were safely on tarmac again.

Repeating something over and over again is what we did at school to learn and I can remember sitting in class with my classmates repeating our multiplication tables over and over again and yes it was chanting. Sometimes when moving from class to class we could hear other pupils 'chanting' their multiplication tables. There was something almost sacred or comforting about that sound and it did help you to learn.

Repeatedly chanting can create a magickal energy and if you have a partner or if you are in a coven, you can chant together which will intensify that energy.

In your ritual, make your chant relevant to your purpose and only for that purpose. Don't stop abruptly, and be sure to close the circle as normal.

Singing

Singing is another form of chanting, probably even more powerful. If you have a beautiful singing voice what nicer way to worship your god? Even if, like me, your voice is not so great – so what? – the joy and energy created by uproarious singing of a melodic tune is a delight and a magickal thing. Most cultures have singing at the heart of worship so if you are able to create Wiccan music do so with a joyful and thankful heart. Singing seems to carry your intentions further. Everything in the universe has a vibration and you have your very own one. Tap into this through music. Be sure to close your circle as normal.

Drumming

The American Indians know that drumming is a very powerful way to create energy in a ritual. Drumming is an important part of Shamanic ritual. Shamans beat drums to reach the spirits. A more Shamanic kind of Wiccan ritual like this is then, less about following a ritual to the letter and more about improvising a little and going with the flow of the energy.

The creation of vibrations can take your ritual intentions far into the universe. A drum circle is joyful and energetic gathering. Some people may have drums, some may clap along, some stamp their feet, some might be moved to hum, sing, whoop or even dance. This may all evolve without the need for words or even music, just the rhythm and vibrations of the drums.

To get the best out of this kind of ritual it is advised to have at least a couple of experienced musicians to ensure that the drumming sounds really good, then let the rest evolve naturally.

If you have neighbours be conscious that this might be too loud to perform without creating a nuisance, and you really don't want a visit from the police threatening you and your group with an ASBO. Keep a look out for anyone who might be feeling faint or a bit overwhelmed by the experience.

Try to keep the ritual's intention focused and, as ever, close the circle when the whole event is over.

Focusing and Visualisation = Chakras

In order to work effectively whether you are 'Drawing Down the Moon' or performing magickal spells or rituals, it is essential that you can focus your attention on what you are doing and visualise your intention. This is not an easy thing to do and for most it only comes with considerable practice. Before you can begin to practise, an understanding of the spiritual workings of your being are essential.

Many of you will have heard of Chakras but may not really understand what they are or how they work. The simplest way to understand Chakras is to think of them as power points within your body.

Although we have within our bodies twenty-one minor Chakras and seven major Chakras, we will focus here on the seven majors.

Each Chakra has its own location, traditional name, common name, colour, and function. Once you are familiar with the location and function of your Chakra points you can begin to practice opening or closing them and this will help you to empower your 'self' and not only improve your ability to focus on your visualisation skills and magickal workings but you will improve life and your health too.

Chakras are centres of psychic energy placed in the central canal of the astral body roughly corresponding to the spinal column in the physical body. I am a Reiki master so I know the importance of the Chakras and their role in healing the body. The Chakras sit at various points between the base of the spine and the top of the head. Two schools of yoga, Tantric and Kundalini, practise meditation on each of them in turn.

See page 159 for methods to achieve meditation.

As you meditate through the Chakras, the latent energy of each one is released, giving you with stronger and stronger sensations of warmth and light at the centre until, when the final meditation is completed, the physical will have merged with the spiritual – the meditator's consciousness merges with the universe.

Each Chakra is like a lotus flower with its very own number of petals, governed by the number of the body channels that conjoin at that point in the astral body. The Base Chakra, also called the *muladhara*, for example is adorned with four petals and it has its own mantra (see page 162 for how to carry out a mantra). Its mantra is '*lam*'. The Sacral Chakra, *svadhishtana*, is six-petalled: its mantra is '*vam*'. The *manipura* or Solar Plexus has ten petals and its mantra is '*ram*'. Next comes the *anahata*, the Heart Chakra with twelve petals and the mantra '*yam*'. Then, with sixteen petals and the mantra '*ham*', is the *vishuddha* or Throat Chakra. The *ajna* Chakra, the Third Eye Chakra with its two petals and the mantra '*om*' is next, followed by the Crown Chakra, the *sahasrara*, or thousand-petal Chakra, which has no mantra.

Anyone wishing to practise this form of meditation would benefit from being taught by an experienced teacher.

Source Chakra

Many consider that the Crown Chakra, located at the top of the head, to be the first Chakra. However, there is an additional Chakra which is located above your head. If you stretch up as high as you can with your dominant hand your fingertips will make a connection to this Chakra. The Source Chakra is where you should start when you begin to meditate or focus your attention. This is the connection to infinity above. If you visualise, a bright white light at the point of the Source Chakra and see, feel, this light coming down into your Crown Chakra you will eventually conquer working with Chakras which in itself will help you to do so many more things. Initially you may find that you can't visualise. Don't worry, try imagining to begin with and gradually your ability to visualise will grow, and develop.

Crown Chakra

This is the centre of our Intelligence:

Traditional Name	Sahasrara
Key word	Knowledge
Flower	Lotus
Location	Top of the head.
Colour	Violet

The Crown Chakra is the centre of our intelligence and knowledge. It is used for gathering information. If it is closed we will not learn anything new and will make no progress in our life.

Third Eye Chakra

This is the centre of our Vision:

Traditional Name	Ajna
Key Word	Visualisation
Flower	Orchid
Location	Centre of the forehead between the eyebrows
Colour	Indigo

This Chakra is associated with the forehead and temples. Stimulated it enhances ESP, clairvoyance, (clear seeing), clairaudience (clear hearing), clairsentience (clear sensing), and visualisation. This is the Chakra that we use to create our future or our intentions.

Throat Chakra

This is the centre of Communication.

Traditional Name	Visuddha
Key word	Communication
Flower	Bluebell
Location	Base of the throat
Colour	Pale blue

This Chakra controls the throat, mouth, ears, neck and governs our ability to listen and speak. This includes listening to our intuition, which in turn helps us to see our goals manifest.

Heart Chakra

This is the centre of Unconditional Love.

Traditional Name	Anahata
Key word	Love
Flower	Rose
Location	Centre of the chest
Colour	Pink or Green

This Chakra is associated with the heart and the entire chest area and is known as the centre for the unconditional love that we share with family friends pets and people whom we love and expect nothing in return.

Solar Plexus Chakra

This is the centre of our strength.

Traditional name	Manipura
Key Word	Power
Flower	Sunflower
Location	Solar plexus
Colour	Yellow to orange

This Chakra is situated in our Solar Plexus right in the middle of our body. This is where men usually demonstrate their strength to their sons when fooling about and they tense up and say 'punch me now' except when my dad did it I punched him on the chin and everybody fell about laughing.

Sacral Chakra

This is the centre of our sexuality.

Traditional name	Svadhisthana
Key Word	Intimacy
Flower	Poppy
Location	Level with the ovaries (lower in men)
Colour	Deep rust to red

This Chakra governs our reproductive system, sexual organs, instinct, awareness, sexuality, and is for sharing sexual love in a committed relationship.

Base Chakra

This is the centre of stability.

Traditional name	Muladhara
Key word	Balance
Flower	Oak tree
Location	Base of the spine
Colour	Dark brown

This Chakra governs our ability to retain or eliminate in any aspect of our life. People who are not grounded can be described as dreamers. People who are too grounded will display depression and despair.

Practice the meditation for Opening Chakras on a regular basis and you will soon find that you can switch on visualisation as fast as snapping your fingers. The colours below are merely suggestions which may help during your meditation exercises. You can use candles in these colours and focus on the candle flame or you can choose crystals in the colour of your choice and use them as an aid to your meditation.

Spell Casting

When you are performing rituals at Sabbats the principle intention is to give thanks and to ask for the blessings for the coming season. Contrary to what is often thought, Wicca and Paganism it is not all about spell casting. Spell casting has its place but should be used to accompany effort. You may wish to perform a spell so that you can get a job or a new job. My first question would be

'What have you done to get a new job?'

If you have done nothing to get a new job and think you will just perform a spell then sit back then you will wait a very long time. The Goddess rewards effort and if no effort is made then there will be no reward. You must do everything that you can and that includes writing letters, cold calling, attending interviews, and anything else that will help you to achieve your desire. The time to cast a spell is when all else has failed and you need the help of the Goddess.

Right Spell / Wrong Spell

My mother always said 'Be careful what you wish for because you might get it and regret it'. In my first book *Book of Spells* I tell a story of a spell that I did to attract love. I hadn't put much thought into it and succeeded in drawing love but ended up hurting the person who was drawn towards me.

If you carry out a spell be very, very careful what you ask for and try to follow these guidelines.

For Love: Do not ask for love from a specific person. That is direct interference in their destiny, life and will. Ask that the right love comes your way.

For Money: Do not ask to be rich as you may become rich through an inheritance and lose someone that you love. It is better to give thank for what you have already been given be ready and open to receive the gifts that are waiting to come to you as blessings from the God and Goddess.

For Success: Do not ask to be successful in any specific venture when you have no way of knowing what the cost will be. The world works in balance and harmony and everything has a price to pay. It is better to ask that you are enabled to give to the best of your ability.

For Career Matters: Do not ask for a specific job, you may get it and hate it once you have it. It is better to ask that the right job will come to you and provide you with job satisfaction and financial gain. I have included verses and rituals for all of the above but if you are using your own then be mindful how you word your verses.

Verses

Witches traditionally speak in rhyme when addressing the God or Goddess during a ritual. At first you may find this difficult to do but if you just clear your mind and let the Lady in she will guide your thoughts and the correct words will come to you.

Your rhymes don't have to be in perfect grammar, they just have to say what you are asking for. See pages 190–200 for verses.

Why not look for the poems of Doreen Valiente for some inspiration too. One of them is in this book (page 201). Doreen wrote many of the verses for the rituals in Gerald Gardner's coven and inspired many more verses written by other Wiccans.

Breaking a Spell

You wouldn't be the first person to make a mistake when creating a spell and I am sure that you won't be the last. This is why it is so important to ensure that you are asking for the right thing in the right manner and always use the words 'An it harm none so mote it be' at the end.

Never-the-less it is important to try to undo any errors because what you put out will for sure come back.

Spell=breaking Blend

Spell-breaking Blend
Equal parts of:
Chili powder
Cinnamon
Galangal
Black pepper
Iron filings
Vetivert.

Blend them together. Wrap in a red pouch and tie with red ribbon and carry with you when you feel the need add the tiniest amount to a charcoal disk and burn during a ritual.

Exorcism and Hex Breaking

Angel	Melchisedek
Bird (picture or ornament)	crow
Colour	black
Creature	wolf
Crystal	clear quartz
Day	Sunday, Monday
Element	Earth
God	Alaunus, Odin, Thoth
Essential oils	eucalyptus, rue, fennel, juniper
Goddess	Kali
Grains	dragon's blood resin, Jerusalem

incense
Metal   Iron
Planet   Mars, Saturn, Moon
Plants and spices   angelica, basil, cayenne, clove,
                                  cumin fumitory, garlic juniper
                                  mustard,   myrrh,   pepper,
                                  peppermint, pine, rosemary, rue,
                                  sage, solomon's seal, spearmint,
                                  St John's wort, thistle, vetivert,
                                  yarrow
Rune   Eihwaz, Wyrd
Tarot Card   Death, Judgement

Runes = Banishing

Delays   Rado (reversed)
Exposure   Peorth (reversed)
Failure   Thurisaz (reversed)
Failure   Uruz (reversed)
Grief   Nauthiz (reversed)
Hastiness   Lagu (reversed)
Poverty   Fehu (reversed)
Property   Othel (reversed)
Relocation   Eoh (reversed)
Saddness   Wunjo (reversed)
Silence   Ansuz (reversed)
Stagnation   Kano (reversed)
Stalker   Mann (reversed)
Sterility   Beork (reversed)
Threats   Eolh (reversed)
Weakness   Tir (reversed)

Tarot Cards = Banishing

Abuse   The Knight of Wands
Conflict   The Five of Swords
Confusion   The Five of Wands
Depression   The Four of Cups

Despair	The Ten of Swords
Disruption	The Tower
Exhaustion	The Nine of Swords
Fear	The Devil
Frustration	The Ten of Wands
Grief	The Three of Swords
Insecurity	The Two of Pentacles
Poverty	The Five of Pentacles
Problems	The Nine of Wands
Theft	The Seven of Swords
Tolerance	The Two of Swords
Restriction	The Eight of Swords
Sadness	The Five of Cups
Sobriety	Temperance
Struggle	The Seven of Pentacles

Magickal Name

Some choose a magickal name that they wish to be known by. I have often been asked what made me choose my name 'Soraya'. I didn't. I am actually named after my grandmother and although the proper spelling and pronunciation was Thouraya, over the years the word became Soraya.

As it so happens my name translated means the 'Brightest Star in the Galaxy of Seven Stars' and the 17th Tarot card in the Major Arcana of the Rider Waite, and several other decks, is indeed a bright star surrounded by seven smaller ones. The interpretation of this card means fame, success, accomplishment, recognition. I don't believe for a minute that this was my parent's intention when they named me. The consonants in my name which are S R Y have numerical values which also add up to 17.

Your magickal name is something that only you should know and the members of your coven if you work in one. The reason for this is fairly simple. Witches believe that your words have power, therefore if someone gossips about you or uses your name to say something bad, the power of these words can act like a hex. Keep your magickal name a secret protected you from harm or negative energies. If you wish to change your name to something that you will be known as then it must be different from your secret name that you would use during rituals, coven work or spell working.

Either way, considerable research should be done into the choosing of your name or names, because they have power. If you are very timid as a person you should choose a strong magical name for example a timid or quiet man might use 'Storm'. A strong woman might use 'Sky'. Try to avoid names of people who have had very bad or difficult lives as your path may then echo theirs. Names of crystals can be effective and the crystal of that type can become a totem stone for you. There are lots to choose from such as Pearl, Ruby, Sapphire, Turquoise, Amber, Jet, Jade, Beryl and Topaz are all nice names and powerful crystals to work with too.

You can experiment with numerology and create or choose a name that has a vibration to suit your purpose. A name that adds up to one will bestow the owner with leadership qualities. For instance

Amber	= 3
Jet	= 8
Jade	= 11
Beryl	= 8
Topaz	= 3

The following graph may help you to choose the right name or names. Once you have decided though you should sleep on it for a few days, perhaps even meditate on it.

1	2	3	4	5	6	7	8	9
A	B	C	D	E	F	G	H	I
J	K	L	M	N	O	P	Q	R
S	T	U	V	W	X	Y	Z	

The numbers in the above names are

A   m   b   e   r
1 + 4 + 2 + 5 + 9 = 21 = 2 + 1 = 3

Add them together and they equal 21 add again and they equal 3

Each number has its own vibration and it is this vibration which lends power both to your Christian name your magickal name and your spell workings. Number can be inscribed on candles for candle magick.

Key Words for Numerology

1 = Power, leadership, beginnings, first.
2 = Mystery, secrets, education, law, medicine
3 = Friendship, celebration, gatherings, contracts, fertility, motherhood.
4 = Stability, security, property, maturity, fatherhood
5 = Construction, engineering, answers, knowledge, uniforms
6 = Lovers, choices, kindness, passion
7 = Control, decisive, spiritual, media,
8 = Strength, power, persistence, focus
9 = Achievement, accomplishment, insight, clarity

The numbers 11 and 22 are considered very powerful in numerology and should in the strictest of terms never be reduced. 11 is the number of Justice and balance and 22 is the number of adventure and courage.

To empower your magickal workings when using these number you can also add the appropriate Tarot card from the major Arcana, The Magician for the number one, The High Priestess for number two etc.

Magickal Tools

Altar

You altar is the space where you will work. For some people this will be a space in their garden. Others may have a whole or part of a room that they use whilst others may only use a small coffee table or space on the floor of their sitting room. Your altar can be as simple or as elaborate as you wish. Its base can be a small table.

Put your altar where it feels right for you, I prefer mine in the centre of my circle. I prefer not to have it on the floor as I would be inclined to trip over it when I am moving. Your altar should allow you to see and access all your tools and magickal accessories

The right side (masculine) of the altar is usually dedicated to the God. Masculine tools are:

a red, yellow, or gold candle,
a statue or figurine
the censor
the wand
the athame
the boline
a dish of salt.

The left half of the altar is usually dedicated to the Goddess (feminine). Feminine tools are:

a silver white or green candle
a statue or figurine
the cup
the pentacle
the bell
crystals
the cauldron
the bowl of water
the besom or broom.

The Athame

An athame is traditionally a double-edged steel knife and the handle is usually black and can be engraved with magickal symbols. You can if you are skilled do this yourself and that is part of the challenge of embarking on your Pagan path. The Athame is masculine and is often immersed into the chalice of wine (feminine) during a Pagan ritual to represent the joining of male and female. There are of course many different traditions; some suggest that your athame should be sharp whilst others suggest that it should be blunt. Some say that you should have a new one made for you so that it holds no other's energies. Others say that you can use a knife that you have come across or whatever suits your purpose. In my opinion you should be guided by your instincts. If you are fortunate enough to afford one to be handmade for you that is fine but if its made for you then it still hold the energies of the craftsman. You will consecrate your ritual tools the first time you use them anyway so it makes no difference whether you have had it made, make it yourself or have received it as a gift or have come across it in a second-hand or antique shop. When I began I used what I had available and later, at a health fair, I came across the most beautiful silver athame and since I knew I was meant to find it and could afford it I had no hesitation in purchasing it.

The Bell

The Bell is feminine and is used like a comma or full stop in a sentence. It is not essential but it is a nice addition to your altar tools. It can be any bell and can be decorated or plain. More important than how your bell looks is how it sounds and it's got to feel right for you. As a Reiki Teaching Master I am in the habit of using Tingshas which are Tibetan chimes. They produce a beautiful sound and awaken the spirit. Tingsha chimes have been used for centuries by Tibetan Buddhists to prepare for meditation. They are a wonderful tool to use for clearing space of negative energies and the healing and balancing of auric fields. In Feng Shui they are used to ring in the four corners of a room in order to open the energy and for clearing spaces.

The Besom or Broomstick

The besom is used primarily as a purifier, and many Wiccan rituals begin by sweeping the area where the sacred circle is to be cast in order to remove any negative energy. The besom can also be used as a protective implement by laying it under the bed, across a windowsill or across the threshold of your property.

The staff of the broom represented the masculine, the phallus, and the head of the broom represented the female. Since the handle was inserted to the twigs this was seen as symbolic of male and female and celebrated fertility and reproduction.

Various traditions were adopted regarding the type of wood that was to be used when making a broom. Some say the handle should be made of ash and birch, broom or hazel for the broom with willow being used to bind the whole together. But you don't need to make your own broom or stick to these components. A broom from a garden centre or hardware store is fine, just make sure that you cleanse it well before you begin to use it.

If you go visiting a friend and you see a broomstick lying across the doorway you will know that a witch is working indoors. This probably stems from the custom of laying the broomstick across the north end of a circle to represent the gateway between the mundane and the spiritual edges of the circle.

Clean your circle both spiritually and physically before you begin by starting in the centre and, moving deosil (clockwise). You can sing or chant as you go and sweep your circle from the centre to the outer edges. While you are doing this you should envision all negativity being swept away. You will find a verse to chant while sweeping the circle further on in this book

Boline

A boline is generally a sharp white handled knife which is used for cutting cords herbs or anything else that you may need it for. They can be crescent shaped, a bit like a sickle. And a curved boline is an especially nice tool for harvesting ceremonial herbs. As it happens, my boline is straight and blunt and never used for cutting however it has a sharp point so I keep it for inscribing magickal symbols onto candles when I am performing candle magick.

Book of Shadows

A book of shadows is simply a journal that you would use to write down all your experiences and, dare I say it, experiments. I use the word experiment because when you first begin your Pagan path it will feel very like experimenting. I am sure that you will try various spells and rituals – you may try messing about with lotions and potions or herbs and grains and at first this will be a confusing process. If you write everything down as you go you won't have to wonder what you did or didn't do. I have received lovely slate books decorated with dragons or cauldrons but they are generally so small that they fill up very quickly. It is better to buy a large lined book to work with and even then you will probably fill that sooner than you would expect. I hate to admit it but my best book of shadows is my computer and you might find that a PC works for you too. If you do decide on a traditional lined book buy one that is spiral bound and then you can fold it back at any page and it will stay open at the page you are working on whereas a hard back book will keep closing over unless you break the spine. You can always have an additional book to keep for posterity, that can be handed down for generations to come. You can decorate it with magickal symbols and art work

Candles

Candles, associated with the element of Fire come in many shapes, sizes and colours and it is a good idea to stock up on a range of colours and sizes so that they are there when you need them. Some prefer to make their own, others insist on beeswax but to be honest the important thing about candles is the colour that you use when performing a spell or ritual. The size is not important either, but some sizes work better than others for instance if I was performing candle magick I would find it difficult to inscribe magickal symbols on a tea light candle. My preference would be a dinner candle.

Altar candles

Altar candles are a variety of candles in assorted sizes used during rituals or religious ceremonies.

One large **white altar candle** is placed on the left of the altar to symbolise the feminine element, the Goddess. You can use a green candle instead.

One large **black altar candle** is placed on the right of the altar to symbolise the masculine element, the God. You can use a red candle instead. These two candles represent balance and harmony just the same as is seen in the yin and yang symbol.

Dinner Candles

Dinner candles are usually about one inch thick and twelve to eighteen inches long. These are available in a multitude of colours including silver which is great for honouring the Goddess and gold, perfect for honouring the God. They come in various shapes from smooth to spiral but smooth are obviously better for candle magick as it is easier to inscribe magickal symbols on smooth surfaces.

One **dinner candle,** representing the element of fire, should be placed at the south section of your table.

God and Goddess Candle

A God and Goddess candle is something that you would make using one black pillar candle and one white pillar candle. The White pillar candle, representing the female should be at least an inch thicker than the black pillar candle which represents the male.

To make your God and Goddess candle start by lighting the white Goddess candle and allow it to burn down until a cavity appears. Sometimes you have to help this process along by manipulating the soft wax. Ones the cavity is about an inch or so deep empty out the melted wax and once it is cool try to fit the black candle into the cavity. You may need to repeat this process several times until the two can fit together. When you have achieved a successful fit, put the candles to one side and keep them until you perform your next Esbat. During your Esbat you can unite the male and female together. To unite the two candles, light the white Goddess candle and allow a pool of wax to form. This will help to lock the two together. Once the pool of wax has formed, at the appropriate time in the ceremony, hold the white Goddess candle in your left hand and the black God candle in your right hand. Hold the two candles aloft, place the black God candle into the cavity of the white Goddess candle as you say

'In this fashion may male and female be joined for the happiness of both. Let the fruits of union give life. Let all be fruitful and let wealth be spread throughout all lands'.

Pillar Candles

Pillar candles range from about two inches in diameter and height to as much as twenty four inches tall. They too come in a variety of colours and they are used for rituals and religious ceremonies although in religious ceremonies they are usually white.

Tea light Candles

Tea light candles are small round candles in a tin holder and these are handy for using in burners or at the 4 quarters in a circle. It is advisable not to leave them unattended as I have experienced the wax catching alight and the candle scorched the dish that it was placed in. I felt quite lucky that no more serious damage was caused. Tea light candles are available scented and unscented but it is better to use the unscented ones for ritual work.

Taper Candles

Taper candles are very slim candles often about ten to two inches long. They are unsuitable for inscribing symbols on for candle magick.

Votive Candles

Votive are small round candles about two inches in height and they must be used in a container such as metal or glass as they melt into oil when they are lit. More often than not they are pre-scented and are used to create ambient atmospheres and diminish unpleasant aromas rather that being used for ritual purposes.

Cauldron

The cauldron represents the Goddess and most witches have or want one. The come in a variety of sizes and I have one which is only two inches tall and I often use it for a variety of magickal or ritual purposes. I also have a traditional black cast iron cauldron which can be used filled with water for scrying or to contain a fire during ceremonies. It can also be used filled with flowers and offerings to the Goddess, to angels and fairies and for the birds (who carry our wishes). It can also be used to hold a lighted candle. Cauldrons especially small ones are useful for containing burning paper during banishing rituals.

Censer and Incense

A censer is a container for burning incense. They are generally made of metal and suspended from chains. They can be difficult to find and are not essential because other incense holders can be just as useful. Some say that the censer represents fire but I prefer to use the candle flame as fire and the censer as air. After all it's the smoke from the burning incense that we are using rather than the burning incense which never actually produces a flame.

Censers can be quite elaborate and expensive but if you pop into any hardware store or gift shop you should be able to find a small brass hanging-plant pot holder complete with chains. Put some salt or sand in the bottom, add a charcoal disc which can be purchased from most New Age shops and, when it is white hot, herbs and grains of crystallised gums can be sprinkled on top. This makes it easy to carry around your circle when you are invoking the element of air. If you find it difficult to obtain the loose incense you can use an incense cone or stick instead. This represents the element of air and should be placed at the east section of your table. If you prefer you can substitute a smudge stick instead. Again these can be purchased from any good New Age shop or you can make your own smudge sticks by drying your favourite herbs and then binding them together in a bunch with some twine.

They can be difficult to use initially because after lighting them it is important to blow on them and fan them to create the smoke. It is also important that they are extinguished properly. I use a small pottery jar half filled with salt and when I am finished I place the glowing end of the smudge stick into the salt and press it down firmly. If you are working indoors remember to check it later to ensure that it has gone out.

Chalice

The cup or chalice is used to hold water, wine, or juice during the ritual. It represents water and is the feminine symbol on the altar. It can be made of silver, brass, copper, or glass or any other natural material.

The cup or chalice is used for symbolically joining the male and female aspects. The cup is feminine and the athame is masculine. At the end of a ritual you would drink your water, wine or fresh juice from the chalice.

Clothing

With or without, the choice is entirely up to you if you are a Solitary witch. However, some traditions or covens insist on being sky clad (naked). Various robes are available on the Internet or if you are handy with a needle and thread you can make your own but you should try to use a natural fabric. Colour and fabric again is your choice if you are a Solitary. If you are in a coven then your group might have specific requirements. If making your own or having someone else making one for you, it can be adorned with magickal symbolism, signs of the zodiac or Pagan symbols.

Cords

Cords are used for Cord Magick, for hand fasting Ceremonies, and used in some traditions as an indication of the priest or priestesses rank or degree. Different ranks are distinguished by the colour of the cord. Most cords used for this purpose are 9 feet long. Different traditions have different requirements regarding the length of cords, the colour of cords and whether or not there should be knots used and if so how many.

Cone of power

A cone of power is not a tool in the tangible sense of the word, however it is a valuable 'tool' in magickal workings. There are several different ways in which to raise the power or energy that we need when working in circle. Raising power is not as difficult as you may think.

The Pentacle

A pentacle is an ancient symbol in the shape of a five-pointed star, which has one point at the top, one each to the left and right and two more at the bottom. The top point of the pentacle points to infinity above and, moving clockwise, the next point symbolises water, the next fire, and the next earth and lastly air. The space in the middle is the space that mankind symbolically occupies. A circle symbolising infinity and protection generally surrounds this five-pointed star.

Some Wiccans wear a pentacle as a piece of jewellery around their neck or on a ring. Some consider the symbol too sacred to be seen by the eyes of other people and always keep it covered. The choice is yours to do as you wish.

The pentacle is always used in circle work, drawn in the air and placed on the altar and this reminds us of the ever-renewing cycles of balance, life, death and rebirth in all aspects. The pentacle can be used for evoking spirits and calling upon the Goddess. Pentacles can be purchased in most New Age shops but can also be made. When I began, my pentacle was hand-painted on an offering plate.

If you have a computer, a simple way to draw one is to open a Microsoft Word document, click on 'insert', and on the drop down menu click on 'picture'. When you have done this a new box titled 'AutoShapes' will appear. Choose the stars and banners icon, click on this, click on the five-pointed star and your pointer on the screen will become a cross. Hold down the left mouse button, press the shift button (this will give you a perfectly proportioned shape) and drag the mouse until the star appears in the size that you want. Print this out and use it as a template to help you draw or paint your own pentacle. If you are artistic, you could even make one from plaster, papier-mâché or wire. Your pentacle should be placed on the centre of your altar.

You should practice drawing a pentacle in the air with your dominant hand.

Start by pointing your right hand at shoulder height downwards to ground level at your left foot, and then draw upwards in an angle to the right and finishing above your head as high as you can reach (this is the top point of the pentacle).

Next draw downwards in a straight line to your right foot then draw upwards to the left, level with your left shoulder; Now draw a straight line across to your right shoulder and then draw down towards the your left foot again finishing where you started. This is an Invoking Pentagram which is the same as a pentacle.

Pentacle Invoking

An invoking pentacle or pentagram is used for many things. It is drawn in the air when casting a circle; it can also be used for clearing negative energy from a room a house or garden, and I use it to bless my car from time to time especially if I am going on a long journey. A pentacle can be used to bless any item, person or situation all the more important to be familiar with drawing its shape in the air. Invoking means bringing toward you.

Pentacle Banishing

Banishing means sending away. Some Pagans or Wiccans use the banishing pentagram which is drawn in the opposite direction to an invoking pentagram. Similarly some will use a banishing pentagram to close a circle whilst others do not. I prefer to close my circle by a statement of intention and by returning the unused elements and energies to the earth. Banishing pentagrams can also be used to dispel negative energy from a situation.

Scourge

A scourge should have a long handle and the tails can be made of any suitable fibre from embroidery threads, ribbon, wool, or any other material. The scourge is symbolic. Everything in life works in balance and harmony: to feel love, one must feel pain; to find, one must lose. The scourge symbolises that there will be some pain involved in discovering the new you and that during this process you may lose friends and loved ones who do not approve of your beliefs. The scourge also assists in the process of concentration or meditation. It is not meant to harm the recipient in any way.

Sword

The sword represents fire and is used for many of the same purposes as the athame and the Staff. The sword can be used for drawing the circle line and fro directing energy. The size and style is up to the individual but you may find them difficult to obtain and work with.

Staff

The staff represents air and is usually around the height of the owner. Staffs are generally decorated with feathers, leather, crystals, carvings or engravings and some are very ornate whilst others are quite plain. As with all magickal tools it is not how they look but more how they are used. Use to direct energy or to draw the circle line.

Wand

The wand is traditionally made of wood although I have made mine from copper pipe filled with crystals with a double terminated crystal at each point. It is a very powerful tool if used correctly. Various woods are used when making your own and if you live near a beach or a forest the best wands can sometimes be found just lying there waiting for you. You can also cut one that appeals to you from a living tree but do so with respect and care.

Some like to have more than one wand to be used for specific purposes but again it is the intention that is important but if you would like to have a variety here are some suggestions.

Apple	love
Ash	healing
Birch	new beginnings
Elder	prophesy
Hawthorn	action
Hazel	wisdom
Willow	insight
Oak	independence
Peach	family and friendship
Cherry	change.

Each sign of the zodiac is associated with a particular tree so if you would like to have a wand that is compatible with your sign the following information will help you:

Aries	Alder
Taurus	Willow
Gemini	Hawthorn
Cancer	Oak
Leo	Holly
Virgo	Hazel
Libra	Vine
Scorpio	Ivy
Sagittarius	Elder
Capricorn	Birch
Aquarius	Rowan
Pisces	Ash

To make your own wand choose a branch that is no longer than the length of your arm from elbow to finger tips. Once you have decided on the branch place that palms of your hands on the tree and silently request that you are granted permission to take this. Once you feel as though your desires have been granted, take a sharp knife, and make a clean cut. When you have done this place the palm of your hands once more on the tree and give silent thanks then bury a small token near the roots. This can be a crystal or a coin or something that has value to you. Your wand or wands may be decorated in any fashion by carving or inscribing them and perhaps using crystals or feathers. Wands are used to raise the energy, to empower it and to direct it.

Other objects

A **table** can be used as your altar.

A large **tray** is required to carry your tools to your circle, whether you are working inside or out, and this can be used as your work surface if you do not have a table.

A **mat** comes in handy for kneeling or sitting on, especially if you are working outside. I use a prayer mat purchased from an Asian store. I remember when I went into the shop to buy it the salesman was not going to let me have it. He asked me if I knew what it was and what it was used for. I managed to convince him that it would be used for a good purpose.

One small pouring **jug** filled with water, representing the element of water, should be placed at the west section of your table.

One small **dish of salt** representing the element of earth should be placed at the north section of your table.

One small **empty dish** should be placed within your reach in front of you to use for blending water and salt during your ceremony.

Your **matches** or **lighter** and candle snuff to put out your candles.

Never, ever blow your candles out or you will undo all your work.

A **towelling cloth** is important for cleaning your hands especially if you are using essential oils for anointing candles.

If you like working with **crystals** or just like having them around you, you can scatter these around your altar.

Magickal Resins

Incense

Incense comes in various shapes and sizes; the most common being sticks, cones but spirals are also available and they are more likely to be used outside in the garden. Both sticks and cones require some sort of holder and they can be carried round a working circle just as easy as a censer can.

Powders Resins and Granules

Incense granules, powders or resins must be burnt in a brass or terracotta holder as they become extremely hot and are difficult to move around once they are lit but of all the scents available granules produce the best variety of perfumes and they are easy to make by your self.

Magical powders can be carried in specially made pouches as well as being burnt on charcoal disks with the addition of resins. Resins have wonderful smells and help the powders to burn. Be careful when using accelerators though as peppers mustards and other sharp smelling spices which on the positive will boost and empower you magickal workings, will also produce a lot of smoke and catch in your throat.

Charcoal Disks

I have often seen people pick these us with a puzzled expression. Charcoal discs are use in conjunction with aromatic resins or grains.

They generally come in a pack of ten wrapped in aluminium foil. They have to be kept very dry. They are inflammable and should be stored safely.

It is suggested that a whole disc be used at a time but in fact I cut mine into quarters and understandably they last longer. They burn at a fierce temperature hence the need for a good fireproof dish and these come in small inexpensive terracotta or for something more elaborate, in brass.

The charcoal disks are quite difficult to light but charcoal tweezers are obtainable and they make life so much easier.

The best way to work with charcoal discs and incense grains is to half fill a small fire proof container with salt or sand. Open the charcoal disc and using a sharp knife split it in two or four pieces. Hold the charcoal disc using the tweezers. If you don't have tweezers place the disc on the salt or sand and very carefully light it with a long match. This may take several attempts but eventually sparks will begin to fly from the charcoal disc and you will begin to smell it.

Blow gently on the area that has caught alight but don't get too close or you will burn yourself. Let the disk sit until it begins to show white patches and that how you will know that it is ready for the addition of your chosen grains. Sprinkle a little pinch of grain, powder or resin or your own combination on the prepared disk and then enjoy being surrounded by the most wonderful aromas.

Some holders have lids which can be placed over the burning charcoal but once covered the disk will stop burning. If you attempt to move a burner of this type be very careful as it will burn through anything it lands on should it fall. Charcoal disks and incense grains, and incense cones can be burnt and carried round a working circle in a censer.

Benzoin Resin
Benzoin resin has a pure, concentrated aroma and is perfect for blending with powders or other resins or grains for a variety of purposes.

Black Diamond
Black Diamond, popular for its spicy fragrance will help to clear negative vibrations.

Camphor Resin
Camphor resin has a very fresh smell and can be used for any ritual involving vitality stimulation and even passion. It can also be used for healing rituals and to restore purpose or direction.

Copal Resin
Copal with its pine and lemon fragrance can be used for purification and love.

Dark Amber
This resin harmonises and balances the senses and helps to reduce stress. It is wonderful for protection, giving and receiving love, and meditation.

Dragons Blood Resin

From the Daemonorops Draco tree, it is so called because the tree is covered in scales and a red shiny resin seeps out between the scales. It can be burned or carried as an aphrodisiac and to banish negativity.

Frankincense

This is one of my all time favourites and has the most beautiful smell. It can be used for almost any sincere purpose and is particularly good for initiations, protection, purification and consecration of altar tools or paraphernalia.

Guggle Resin

Similar in Its qualities to Myrrh Guggle can be used in healing spells and for protection, triumph, strength, and excelling In sports or competitions.

Myrrh

Myrrh, regarded by many as sacred, will amplify any other resin or powder or Indeed any ritual or spell. It can be used for almost any special purpose especially purifying and consecrating and is wonderful used as an aid to meditation.

Pine Resin

Pine resin is perfect for purifying, cleansing and stimulation and can be mixed with other resins or powders to boost their properties or purpose. It is said to increase fertility.

Sandalwood Powder

Sandalwood is wonderful for marriage passion love and romance and can be added to other blends to empower these qualities.

Sandarac Resin

With its warm frankincense-like fragrance Sandarac has very relaxing properties and can e used in healing spells or rituals. It is said that Sandarac was the gift of gold to the infant Jesus.

Storax Resin

With its floral fragrance Styrax can be used for spring rituals, romance and friendship or added to other resins or powders to lift them.

Tonka Beans

Fragrant Tonka Beans add subtle tones to any blend of powders and can be used for romance love passion, relaxation and peace.

Magickal Powders

Magickal powders are probably the easiest things to make and you can tailor them to suit any spell or ritual. You can use dried petals or seeds, herbs, essential oils, dried and chopped roots, dried or chopped seaweed, grains, or dried twigs, pretty much anything. I use chalk as an ingredient because I can obtain them easily and powder the appropriate colour in a pestle and mortar whenever I need them. I also have a spare coffee grinder that I keep and only use for mixing magickal powders.

Save an old pillowcase and cut it into squares measuring about 6 inches by 6 inches and when you have combined your chosen ingredients put a scoopful in the middle of the cotton square, gather the corners together and then tie the pouch with a ribbon of the appropriate colour.

Red - life, vitality, health
Pink -love
Blue - healing, peace, spirituality
Black - endings, negation of ego
Green - growth, creativity, wealth
Orange - optimism, joy
Yellow - thought, mental activity
Purple - power, assertion, confidence
White - spirituality, protection.

When you have made your magickal powder you can use it as a charm for its intended purpose carrying it in your bag or pocket or you can use them during spell working or rituals by sprinkling the contents on a charcoal disk.

You can also scatter the powders around your home garden workplace or your circle to empower your intention.

Magickal Powder Blends

To make magickal powders, blend together any of the following suggestions or create your own. If you don't have a particular flower herb or seed you can substitute it with a few drops of essential oil. Once you have created or mixed your blend, label and store in an airtight jar until required. These powders can be scattered around your circle, home place of work or business, your car or anywhere that you feel they will benefit your intention. They can be carried in a pouch made of an appropriate colour and tied with ribbon, natural twine or cord.

To burn your magickal powders add a small amount of resin from the Magickal Resins section and store in the same way until required. The resin will aid the burning process and enhance the perfume and the energy depending on what you use.

Accelerator Blend
Accelerator blends are used to boost and hasten any magickal rituals or spells. Blend together equal parts of Basil, cinnamon, clover, ginger, black pepper and tea leaves. Wrap in a red square and tie with a red ribbon or string to carry with you to empower any working spell.

To burn on charcoal; add a very small amount of resin of your choice from the list on page 125.

Concentration and Study
Vetivert, nutmeg, allspice sage and clary sage.

Confidence
Violet and vetivert.

Creativity
Lilac, cinnamon and honeysuckle.

Divination and Prophesy
Cinnamon, cardamom, coriander, orris, vetivert cinnamon, sandalwood, clove, myrrh yarrow, eyebright, lemongrass, mugwort, rose petals.

Fertility
Cinnamon, sage, rose.

Forgiveness
Red peppercorns, rose, jasmine, sandalwood.

Friendship
Lily, hyacinth, lemon rose, mint.

Happiness
Lavender, catnip, marjoram.

Healing
Orris, vanilla, clove, lavender.

Health
Eucalyptus, myrrh, thyme, allspice.

Home and family
Dragon's blood, gardenia, blossoms, lavender, meadowsweet, olive leaves, passion flower, purslane, rose petals.

Legal
Mix together some of the Accelerator blend and add to it any herb or spice that suits your legal purpose. For example for property add any of the following myrrh resin, incense beans, elderflower, heather, lavender, oak, olive, rowan, Solomon's seal, tea.

Love
Basil, orris, rose petals, vetivert, yarrow, ginger, rose petals, basil, lavender gardenia, lilac, lily of the valley, lily.

Loyalty
Lime, orange or peach or apple blossom, clove, allspice, mullein, sage.

Luck
Vanilla, cinnamon, clover, heather.

Magickal Components for Rituals

Balance

Angel	Uriel
Bird (picture or ornament)	humming bird
Colours	blue, indigo, violet, yellow
Creatures (picture or ornament)	camel, dolphin, dragon, elephant, fox, horse, lizard, otter, spider
Crystals	amazonite, blue lace agate, chrysocolla, citrine coral, diamond emerald moss agate
Day	Monday
Element	earth
Essential oils	basil, benzoin, clove, hyssop
Gods	Forseti, Raiden, Tiwaz
Goddess	Isis, Maat
Grains	Jerusalem incense
Metal	lead
Planet	Venus
Plants, or, spices	chamomile, calendula, lemon, balm, red, clover
Rune	Eihwaz, Eoh, Gefu, Gera, Inguz (upright)
Tarot card	The High Priestess

Beauty

Angel	Zuriel, Hael, Yofiel
Bird (picture or ornament)	magpie, peacock
Colour	red
Creature (picture or ornament)	butterfly, chameleon, oyster, dolphin, leopard, lion, lynx, panther, spider
Crystal	amber, opal, spinel
Day	Friday, Monday
Element	water

Essential oils	rose, melissa, honeysuckle, lotus
God	Maponos, Adonis, Apollo, Midir
Goddess	Aphrodite, Ariadne, Belisama, Freya, Hathor, Hebe, Hera, Isis
Grains	myrrh
Metal	copper, silver
Planet	Jupiter, Moon, Pluto, Sun, Venus
Plants and spices	angelica, bluebell, borage, celandine, gardenia, hyacinth, lilac, magnolia, narcissus, orchid, rose
Rune	Beork, Inguz, (upright)
Tarot card	The Sun, The Star

Business/Legal

Angel	Michael
Bird (picture or ornament)	jackdaw, magpie, raven
Colour	red
Creature (picture or ornament)	ferret, hare, rat, salmon, snail, stag
Crystal	bloodstone, citrine, jasper, malachite
Day	Saturday, Sunday, Thursday, Tuesday, Wednesday
Element	earth
Essential	benzoin, basil
Essential oils	hyssop
God	Cissonius, Weland
Goddess	Clota, Dea, Sequana, Erecura, Rosmerta
Grains	amber, powder
Metal	iron
Planet	Jupiter, Mars, Mercury, Sun
Plants and spices	celandine, cinquefoil, marigold
Rune	Daeg, Gefu, Gera, Wunjo (upright)
Tarot card	The High Priest, The Three Pentacles, The Three Wands

Caution

Angel	Gabriel
Bird (picture or ornament)	crow
Colour	red
Creature (picture or ornament)	snail, spider
Crystal	chrysoprase
Day	Friday
Element	fire
Essential oils	hyssop, benzoin, peppermint
God	Orion, Abandinus, Lugus, Mimir
Goddess	Ariadne, Athena, Freya, Hecate, Hestia, Isis, Morrigan, Nuit
Grains	benzoin
Metal	steel
Planet	Mercury
Plants and spices	nettle, thistle
Rune	Is, Lagu, Nauthiz, Thurisaz (upright)
Tarot card	The Four Swords

Clarity and Insight

Angel	Jophiel, Metatron, Sachael
Bird (picture or ornament)	eagle, hawk, owl
Colour	white
Creature	ferret, fox, hare, leopard, lion, lynx, otter, rat
Crystal	blue lace agate, selenite
Day	Monday
Element	water
Essential oils	hyssop, birch, angelica, clary sage, eucalyptus, lemon
God	Odin
Goddess	Amaterasu, Ariadne, Coventina, Vesta
Grains	myrrh, resin, dragon's blood resin, Jerusalem incense
Metal	brass, platinum

Planet	Mercury
Plants and spices	oak
Rune	Ansuz (upright)
Tarot card	The Moon, The Hermit

Communication

Angel	Ecanus, Jehoel, Ongkanon
Bird (picture or ornament)	crow, hawk, parrot
Colour	yellow
Creature	cockerel, dolphin, spider
Crystal	celestite, chrysocolla, danburite, malachite, moldavite, moss, agate
Day	Friday, Wednesday
Element	air
Essential oils	caraway, chamomile
God	Bragi
Goddess	Iris
Grains	gum arabic, resin
Metal	silver
Planet	Mercury, Jupiter, Mars, Sun
Plants and spices	bluebell, caraway, dill, lavender, lemon, verbena, marjoram
Rune	Ansuz (upright)
Tarot card	The Knight Cups (emotional), The, Knight Pentacles (financial)

Compassion

Angel	Gabriel
Bird (picture or ornament)	dove
Colour	white
Creature	dog
Crystal	carnelian, celestite
Day	Friday
Element	water
Essential oils	cypress
God	Baldr

Goddess	Ariadne, Arnemetia, Frigga
Grains	Jerusalem incense
Metal	silver
Planet	Moon, Neptune, Venus
Plants and spices	basil, elder, flower, hawthorn, lotus, marjoram, myrrh, pennyroyal rue, willow, yew
Rune	Mann (upright)
Tarot card	The Six of Cups

Concentration and Study

Angel	Dina
Bird (picture or ornament)	owl, turkeys
Colour	white, oran, yellow
Creature (picture or ornament)	crab, ferret, goat, leopard, lion, lizard, salmon, snail, spider, tortoise
Crystal	danburite, emerald
Day	Saturday, Wednesday
Element	air, earth
Essential oils	petitgrain, lavender, pennyroyal, black, pepper, rosemary, thyme
God	Cissonius, Weland
Goddess	Don
Grains	dragon's blood resin
Metal	platinum, silver
Planet	Jupiter
Plants, and spices	borage
Rune	Gera (no reverse)
Tarot card	The Ten of Pentacles

Confidence

Angel	Malchediel
Bird (picture or ornament)	raven
Colour	indigo, red, violet, yellow
Creature (picture or ornament)	elephant, goat, horse, leopard, salmon
Crystal	citrine, moss, agate

Day	Thursday
Element	fire
Essential	benzoin
Essential oils	hyssop, lavender, petitgrain
God	Cissonius, Thor
Goddess	Athena
Grains	amber, powder
Metal	gold
Planet	Jupiter, Mars, Mercury
Plants and spices	beans, eyebright, sunflower
Rune	Tir (upright)
Tarot card	The Chariot

Courage

Angel	Malchediel
Bird (picture or ornament)	eagle
Colour	red, yellow
Creature (picture or ornament)	leopard, lion, salmon, wolf
Crystal	bloodstone, diamond, lapis lazuli, sardonyx, tiger, eye, turquoise
Day	Saturday
Element	fire
Essential oils	black, pepper, yarrow, thyme, ginger
God	Orion, Freyr, Herne, Odin, Ragnarok, Tiwaz, Zeus
Goddess	Agrona, Andraste, Arduinna, Artio
Grains	dragon's blood resin
Metal	gold
Planet	Jupiter, Mars, Sun
Plants and spices	basil, beans, borage, chives, columbine, honeysuckle, horseradish, nettle, pepper, thyme
Rune	Tir, Uruz (upright)
Tarot card	The Fool

Creativity

Angel	Liwet, Raphael
Bird (picture or ornament)	owl, seagull
Colour	orange
Creature	ants, hare, salmon spider
Crystal	aventurine, carnelian, celestite, rose quartz
Day	Friday, Monday
Element	fire
Essential oils	petitgrain, thyme, star, anise
God	Herne, Bragi, Helios, Hephaestus
Goddess	Bast, Belisama, Brigid, Cerridwen, Dea, Sequana, Demeter
Grains	Jerusalem incense
Metal	brass
Planet	Mars, Mercury, Sun, Uranus, Venus
Plants and spices	acorns, beans, beech, lily, mistletoe
Rune	Inguz (upright)
Tarot card	Eight of Pentacles, The Magician

Divination and Prophesy

Angel	Gabriel, Uriel, Raziel
Bird (picture or ornament)	crow, raven
Colour	indigo, violet
Creature	cat, ferret, panther, spider, wolf
Crystal	alexandrite, amethyst, lapis lazuli, moldavite, sodalite
Day	Sunday, Monday
Element	water
Essential oils	lemongrass, yarrow, star, anise, honeysuckle, clary sage, cinnamon, nutmeg, orange, jasmine, pine, sage
God	Odin, Thoth
Goddess	Athena, Brighid, Cerridwen, Freya, Hathor
Grains	myrrh, resin, amber, powder, dragon's

	blood resin, frankincense, Jerusalem incense
Metal	copper, silver
Planet	Sun, Mercury, Moon, Neptune
Plants and spices	anise, clove, eyebright, fumitory, galangal root, juniper, lavender, sage, thyme, tobacco, vervain, yarrow
Rune	Eihwaz, Wyrd (no reverse)
Tarot card	The Hanged Man, The Moon

Fertility

Angel	Lailah
Bird (picture or ornament)	stork
Colour	red
Creature	fish, goose, ram, salmon
Crystal	calcite, carnelian, coral, geodes, moonstone
Day	Friday
Element	earth
Essential oils	vanilla absolute, lily, patchouli
God	Baldr, Cernunnos, Freyr, Geb, Osiris
Goddess	Arianrod, Artemis, Athena, Aufaniae, Dea, Matrona, Freya, Frigga, Selkhet
Grains	frankincense
Metal	copper
Planet	Moon, Sun, Venus
Plants and spices	acorns, apple, banana, beans, cuckoo, flower, dates, hawthorn, hazelnuts, mistletoepomegranate, seeds, poppy
Rune	Beork (upright)
Tarot card	The Empress, The Ace of Wands

Forgiveness

Angel	Charmeine
Bird (picture or ornament)	owl
Colour	violet

Creature	dog, dolphin, wolf
Crystal	jade, tiger, eye, turquoise
Day	Sunday
Element	water
Essential	benzoin, lily, chamomile, rosemary
God	Baldr
Goddess	Rhiannon
Grains	frankincense
Metal	aluminium, tin, silver
Planet	Venus
Plants and spices	poppy, sage, Solomon's seal
Rune	Beork, Daeg (upright)
Tarot card	The Six of Cups

Freedom

Angel	Colopatiron, Malchedie, Zacharael
Bird (picture or ornament)	eagle, humming, bird
Colour	yellow
Creature	butterfly, cat, crab, dolphin, elephant, goat, grasshopper, leopard, wolf
Crystal	calcite
Day	Tuesday
Essential oils	petitgrain, bergamot, cajuput, hyssop
Element	fire
God	Baldr, Tiwaz
Goddess	Ariadne, Feronia
Grains	frankincense
Metal	gold
Planet	Mars, Mercury
Plants and spices	angelica, strawberry, self heal, lady's mantle
Rune	Beork (upright)
Tarot card	The Eight Cups, The Two of Wands

Friendship

Angel	Hael, Mihr

Bird (picture or ornament)	bluebird, cuckoo, dove, robin
Colour	yellow
Creature	dog, dolphin, donkey, elk, horse, wolf
Crystal	chrysoprase, diamond, jasper, selenite, turquoise
Day	Friday, Wednesday
Essential oils	geranium, lily, plumeria, marjoram, chamomile
Lemon	verbena, orange
Element	water
God	Baldr, Odin
Goddess	Clota, Hestia, Isis, Frigga, Vesta
Grains	frankincense
Metal	silver
Planet	Sun, Venus, Mercury
Plants and spices	beans, bluebell
Rune	Ansuz, Gefu (no reverse)
Tarot card	The Knight of Cups, The Knight of Pentacles

Grounding

Angel	Gabriel
Bird (picture or ornament)	peacock, turkey
Colour	yellow
Creature	bull, camel
Crystal	hematite, kunzite, obsidian, onyx, tiger, eye
Day	Saturday
Element	earth
God	Forseti, Raiden, Tiwaz
Goddess	Isis
Essential oils	hyssop, angelica, vetiver
Grains	dragon's blood resin
Metal	iron, silver
Planet	Saturn
Plants and spices	angelica, beans, bluebell
Rune	Is, Ansuz, Gefu (no reverse)

Tarot card	Temperance

Gratitude

Angel	Ooniemme, Shemael, Uzziel
Bird (picture or ornament)	dove
Colour	gold
Creature	dog
Crystal	clear quartz, amethyst
Day	Monday
Element	water
Essential oils	tea-tree, geranium, rose, pennyroyal, fennel
God	Lugh
Goddess	Frigga, Isis
Grains	sandalwood
Metal	gold, silver
Planet	Jupiter
Plants and spices	apple, banana, barley, beans
Rune	Wunjo, Fehu, Ansuz (upright)
Tarot card	The Sun, The Six of Pentacles

Happiness and Joy

Angel	Camael, Gabriel
Bird (picture or ornament)	humming, bird
Colour	orange
Creature	salmon
Crystal	chrysocolla, chrysoprase, citrine, danburite, lapis lazuli, rose quartz, ruby, sardonyx
Day	Friday, Sunday
Element	fire
Essential oils	geranium, orange, neroli, bergamot, hyacinth, rose, geranium
God	Freyr
Goddess	Frigga
Grains	amber, powder

Metal	gold
Planet	Sun, Venus
Plants and spices	celandine, hyacinth, myrtle, sweet, pea
Rune	Daeg, Inguz, Wunjo
Tarot card	The Sun, The Nine of Cups, The Ten of Cups

Healing and Health

Angel	Izra'il, Mumiah, Raphael, Sariel
Bird (picture or ornament)	dove
Colour	green, pink
Creature	chameleon, fish
Crystal	almost all crystals
Day	Monday (during Imbolc)
Essential oils	carnation, hops, rue, pennyroyal, coriander, thyme, spearmint, tea-tree, eucalyptus, juniper, fennel, pine, lemon, sandalwood, lavender, cypress, fir, manuka
Element	earth, water
God	Alaunus, Baldr, Lenus
Goddess	Brigid, Hathor, Isis, Pritona, Sekhmet, Vesta
Grains	amber, benzoin, gum arabic, resin, Jerusalem incense
Metal	copper, silver
Planet	Neptune, Sun, Venus
Plants and spices	angelica, cinnamon, coriander, cowslip, eucalyptus, fennel, feverfew, garlic, ginseng, juniper, lavender, mint, self heal, mustard, myrrh, nutmeg, peppermint, pine, poppy, rosemary, sage, spearmint, st., John's, wort, thyme
Rune	Sigel (upright)
Tarot card	The Ten of Cups

Home and Family

Angel	Rehael, Shekinah, Zuriel
Bird (picture or ornament)	geese, chickens, turkey,
Colour	green
Creature	cat, dog, wolf
Crystal	geodes
Day	Friday
Element	earth
Essential oils	geranium, thyme, pennyroyal, plumeria, cardamom, myrtle, tea-tree
God	Fenrir
Goddess	Hecate, Hestia, Vesta
Grains	amber, powder, frankincense, myrrh, resin, incense
Metal	copper, gold, silver
Planet	Sun, Venus
Plants and spices	angelica, apple, bluebell, celandine, chamomile, cinquefoil, elder, flower, jasmine, lady's, mantle, laurel, lavender, neroli, orange, plantain, rosemary, rowan, sunflower, sweet pea
Rune	Eolh (upright)
Tarot card	The Four of Wands, The Ten of Cups, The Ten of Pentacles

Hope

Angels	Perpetiel
Bird (picture or ornament)	swan
Colour	white
Creature	butterfly, dolphin, salmon
Crystal	amazonite, calcite, citrine
Day	Friday
Element	air
Essential oils	pennyroyal, frangipani
God	Odin, Orion
Goddess	Ariadne

Grains	benzoin
Metal	gold, silver
Planet	Jupiter, Mars, Neptune, Pluto, Sun, Venus
Plants and spices	beans, bluebell, sunflower
Rune	Daeg, Inguz, Kano (upright)
Tarot card	The Star

Justice

Angel	Gabriel, Israfil, Munkir, Nemamiah
Bird (picture or ornament)	crow
Colour	silver, white
Creature	lion, wolf
Crystal	diamond
Day	Monday
Element	fire
God	Forseti, Raiden, Tiwaz
Goddess	Themis
Grains	Jerusalem incense
Metal	copper
Planet	Mars, Venus
Plants and spices	elderflower, eucalyptus, rowan, Solomon's seal
Rune	Inguz, Sigel, Uruz, Wunjo (upright)
Tarot card	Judgement, Justice

Love and Handfasting

Angel	Gabriel, Hadraniel, Shekinah
Bird (picture or ornament)	goldfinch, swan
Colour	pink
Creature	dolphin
Crystal	alexandrite, amber, bloodstone, emerald, jade, malachite, moonstone, pearl, rose quartz, sapphire, herkimer, diamond

Day	Friday
Element	water
Essential oils	cardamom, hyacinth, ylang-ylang, rose, coriander, white, ginger, jasmine, yarrow, rosemary, palmarosa, ginger, lavender, rose
God	Adonis, Cupid, Osiris
Goddess	Aphrodite, Ariadne, Brighid, Freya, Isis, Vesta
Grains	frankincense
Metal	copper, silver
Planet	Sun, Venus
Plants and spices	angelica, apple, chickweed, clover, gardenia, ginger, hibiscus, ivy, jasmine, lavender
Rune	Gefu, Inguz, Mann (upright)
Tarot card	The Lovers, The Two of Cups, The Ace of Cups, The Ten of Cups, The Night of Cups

Luck

Angel	Israfel
Bird (picture or ornament)	geese, goldfinch, lark, martin, owl
Colour	yellow
Creature	cat, pig, spider
Crystal	alexandrite, amber, aventurine, pyrite, turquoise
Day	Friday, Monday, Sunday
Element	earth
Essential	sandalwood, frankincense, juniper, clove
God	Odin
Goddess	Fortuna
Grains	amber, powder
Metal	tin
Planet	Jupiter, Sun, Venus
Plants and spices	anise, beans, hollyhock, lily, sunflower,

	carnation, shamrock, white, heather, clover
Rune	Sigel (upright)
Tarot card	The Ten of Cups (emotional), The Ten of Pentacles (material)

Passion

Angel	Cherubim
Bird (picture or ornament)	love, bird, (picture or ornament)
Colour	red
Creature	bull
Crystal	calcite, sunstone, bloodstone
Day	Friday, Tuesday
Element	fire
Essential oils	cardamom, ylang-ylang, jasmine, neroli, patchouli, ginger, cinnamon, pine, sandalwood, vanilla absolute, camphor, ginger, jasmine, patchouli, neroli
God	Cernunnos, Cupid, Freyr
Goddess	Aphrodite, Demeter, Freya
Grains	benzoin
Metal	iron
Planet	Mars, Sun, Venus, Juniper
Plants and spices	hibiscus, lemongrass, parsley, patchouli, peppermint, tuberose, vanilla
Rune	Inguz, (upright)
Tarot card	The Knight of Swords, The Ace of Swords, The Ace of Wands

Peace

Angel	Charmeine, Gavree, Melchisedek, Valoel
Bird (picture or ornament)	dove
Colour	blue

Creature	dolphin
Crystal	aquamarine, blue, lace, agate, celestite, jet, kunzite, moldavite, moonstone, obsidian, apache teardrop (obsidian), rhodocrosite, rose quartz
Day	Sunday
Element	water
Essential oils	jasmine, white, ginger, hyacinth, hops, rue, basil, lavender, ylang-ylang, lily, lemon, balm, plumeria, bergamot, chamomile, rose
God	Baldr, Forseti
Goddess	Eirene, Isis, Pax
Grains	myrrh
Metal	platinum, silver, steel
Planet	Moon, Venus
Plants and spices	basil, borage, clary sage, carnation, gardenia, jasmine, lavender, lemon, balm, lilac, magnolia, meadowsweet, myrrh, olive
Rune	Eihwaz
Tarot card	The Six Of Cups, The Ten Of Cups

Power

Angel	Sandalphon
Bird (picture or ornament)	eagle, falcon
Colours	gold, red
Creatures	ants, ape, boar, bull, elephant, horse, tiger, lion, panther, salmon, wolf
Crystal	malachite, moldavite, opal, quartz, ruby, sapphire, staurolite
Day	Thursday, Tuesday
Element	fire
Essential oils	lime, dill, yarrow, thyme, camphor, vanilla absolute, saffron, carnation, orange
God	Thor, Odin, Zeus

Goddess	Arduinna, Freya, Isis, Sif, Sunna
Grains	dragon's blood resin
Metal	brass, copper, silver
Planet	Jupiter, Mars, Sun, Uranus
Plants and spices	beans, ivy, cedar, garlic, ginger, ginseng, mustard, nettle, oak, pine, rowan, Solomon's seal, St John's wort, sunflower, thistle
Rune	Eihwaz, Hagal, Fehu (upright)
Tarot card	Strength, Ace of Swords

Property

Angel	Zuphlas
Bird (picture or ornament)	housemartin
Colour	brown, green
Creature	horse
Crystal	diamond
Day	Monday
Element	earth
God	Terminus
Goddess	Clota, Dea, Sequana, Erecura, Rosmerta
Grains	myrrh, resin, incense
Metal	iron
Planet	Saturn
Plants and spices	beans, elderflower, heather, lavender, oak, olive, rowan, Solomon's seal, tea
Rune	Eoh, Othel (upright)
Tarot card	The Emperor, The High Priest

Prosperity

Angel	Jamaerah
Bird (picture or ornament)	magpie, peacock, swan
Colour	gold, green, red
Creature	bees, bull, cattle, cow, dragon, elephant, goose, horse, porcupine,

	snail, trout
Crystal	bloodstone, chrysoprase, citrine, emerald, jade, opal, pearl, peridot, pyrite, ruby, sapphire, spinel, staurolite, topaz, turquoise
Day	Sunday, Thursday
Essential oils	lemon, balm, yarrow, basil, vetivert, nutmeg, cinnamon, honeysuckle, saffron, oakmoss, ginger, vanilla, tuberose
Element	earth
God	Cissonius, Math, Njord
Goddess	Damona, Dana, Dea, Sequana, Erecura, Fortuna, Freya, Hecate, Isis
Grains	amber, powder
Metal	brass, copper, silver, tin
Planet	Pluto, Sun
Plants and spices	allspice, almond, anise, beans, cashew, cinnamon, clove, clover, ginseng, juniper, moss, myrtle, pomegranate, tea, thyme, wheat
Rune	Fehu (upright)
Tarot card	The Magician, The Nine of Pentacles, The Four of Pentacles

Protection

Angel	Gavree, Herchel, Verchiel
Bird (picture or ornament)	eagle, pheasant
Colour	black, gold
Creature (picture or ornament)	alligator, ants, ape, beetle, boar, bull, crab, crocodile, dragon, elk, hedgehog, tortoise, wolf
Crystal	agate, amber, apache teardrop (obsidian), beryl, celestite, chalcedony, chrysoprase, coral, diamond, jade, lapis lazuli, malachite, moonstone, obsidian, onyx, petrified, wood, quartz,

	sardonyx, serpentine, staurolite, sunstone, tiger, eye, topaz, turquoise
Day	Saturday
Element	fire
Essential oils	lime, vetivert, spearmint, black, pepper, geranium, pine, juniper, chamomile, bay, cinnamon
God	Abandinus, Anubis, Aries, Dagda, Odin, Tiwaz
Goddess	Agrona, Ariadne, Artio, Athena, Freya, Hecate, Hestia, Isis, Morrigan
Grains	amber powder, dragon's blood resin frankincense
Metal	gold, iron, lead, silver, steel
Planet	Jupiter, Mars, Saturn, Sun
Plants and spices	angelica, anise, basil, bay, bergamot, black, pepper, burdock, caraway, cedar, cinnamon, clove, comfrey, cumin, cypress, dill, eucalyptus, eyebright, galangal root, garlic, holly, mandrake, marigold, marjoram, mint, mistletoe, mugwort, myrrh, nettle, oak, orris root, pepper, peppermint, pine, rowan, rue, sage, Solomon's seal, thistle, valerian
Rune	Eihwaz, Eolh (upright)
Tarot card	Temperance

Purification

Angel	Shushienae
Bird (picture or ornament)	swan
Colour	green
Creature (picture or ornament)	butterfly, frogs
Crystal	aquamarine
Day	Monday
Element	fire
Element	water

Essential, oils	lime, geranium coriander, cypress, peppermint, lemongrass, fennel, yarrow, lemon, verbena, camphor, eucalyptus, woodruff, citronella, nutmeg, lemon, pine, dill, juniper, white, ginger, lemon, balm
God	Alaunus, Ra
Goddess	Cailleach, Cloacina
Grains	copal, myrrh, benzoin, dragon's blood resin, frankincense, Jerusalem incense
Metal	gold, silver
Planet	mars, sun
Plants and spices	angelica, anise, basil, bergamot, cedar, chamomile, cinnamon, clove, dill, elder, flower, eucalyptus, fennel, ginger, jasmine, juniper, lavender, lemon, lime, lemon, verbena, mandrake, mint, mistletoe, myrrh, myrtle, nutmeg, oak, orange, parsley, peppermint, pine, rosemary, rowan, sage, thistle, valerian
Rune	Beork (upright)
Tarot card	Temperance

Remembrance

Angel	Sofiel, Elijah, Ezekiel, Sammael
Bird (picture or ornament)	dove
Colour	white
Creature (picture or ornament)	elephant
Crystal	coral
Day	Thursday
Element	earth
Essential oils	coriander, hyacinth, melissa, rosemary, yarrow, bergamot, amyris, rosewood
God	Odin
Goddess	Hathor
Grains	Jerusalem incense

Metal	iron
Planet	moon
Plants and spices	anise, basil, bluebell, elder, flower, hawthorn, lotus, mandrake, marjoram, myrrh, parsley, pennyroyal, pine, poplar, poppy, rosemary, rue, thyme, violet, willow, yew
Rune	Wyrd (no reverse)
Tarot card	temperance, eight, cups, ten, cups

Sobriety

Angel	Tabbris
Bird (picture or ornament)	swallow
Colour	white
Creature	(picture or ornament) wolf
Crystal	amethyst
Day	Saturday
Element	water
Essential oils	camphor, cypress, nutmeg, carnation, cedar
God	Tiwaz
Goddess	Ananita
Grains	gum arabic, resin
Metal	iron, silver
Planet	Mercury
Plants and spices	anise, clove, elderflower, hawthorn, sage
Rune	Tir (upright)
Tarot card	Temperance, The Eight of Cups, The Wheel

Spirituality

Angel	Zadkiel, Micah, Nathaniel
Bird (picture or ornament)	eagle
Colour	indigo, violet

Creature (picture or ornament)	bear, cow, dolphin, lizard, panther, wolf
Crystal	carnelian, diamond, moldavite, moonstone, sugilite
Day	Monday, Thursday
Element	fire, water
Essential oils	sandalwood, jasmine, cedar, rosewood, frankincense, myrrh, bergamot, carnation, chamomile, myrrh, niaouli
God	Odin
Goddess	Sekhmet
Grains	copal, dragon's blood resin, Jerusalem incense
Metal	iron
Planet	Jupiter, Mercury, Moon
Plants and spices	anise, borage, cinnamon, elder, flower, iris, sage
Rune	Eihwaz
Tarot card	The Hermit

Strength

Angel	Rampel, Tabbris, Zuphlas
Bird (picture or ornament)	falcon
Colour	gold
Creature (picture or ornament)	ants, ape boar, camel, goat horse, leopard, lion, salmon, wolf
Crystal	amber, bloodstone, diamond, garnet
Day	Thursday
Element	fire
Essential oil	carnation, nutmeg
God	Orion, Alisanos, Bran, Cernunnos, Tyr
Goddess	Arduinna
Grains	dragon's blood resin
Metal	iron
Planet	Venus
Plants and spices	oak, cypress, horse, chestnut, poplar,

	sage, willow
Rune	Tir (upright)
Tarot card	Strength

Success

Angel	Perpetiel
Bird (picture or ornament)	goldfinch, pheasant
Colour	gold, red
Creature (picture or ornament)	camel, elephant, goat, lion, salmon, spider
Crystal	amazonite, chrysoprase
Day	Sunday
Element	fire
Essential oils	nutmeg, woodruff
God	Búri, Herne, Lugh
Goddess	Agrona, Clota
Grains	amber, powder, frankincense
Metal	gold, platinum, silver
Planet	Jupiter, Mars, Sun
Plants and spices	allspice, almond, beans, cedar, celandine, chamomile, cinnamon, clove, clover, comfrey, dill, elder, flower, fenugreek, galangal root, ginger, horse, chestnut, jasmine, mandrake, marigold, mint, myrtle, nutmeg, oak, orange, oregano, parsley, rowan, sunflower
Rune	Gefu, Inguz, Tir, Uruz, Wunjo
Tarot card	The Star

Travel

Angel	Elemiah
Bird (picture or ornament)	eagle, lapwing, swallow
Colour	green
Creature (picture or ornament)	ants, donkey, elephant, ferret, goat, leopard, wolf

Crystal   chalcedony
Day   Thursday, Tuesday
Element   air, earth water
Essential, oil   saffron, fennel, frankincense
God   Hermes
Goddess   Hecate, Tara
Grains   Jerusalem incense
Metal   aluminium, gold, silver, tin
Planet   Jupiter, Mars, Mercury, Sun
Plants and spices   caraway, comfrey, daffodil, feverfew,
                                       garlic, heather, juniper, mint,
                                       mistletoe, moss, mugwort, mustard,
                                       oak, pennyroyal, rowan, rue,
                                       strawberry, self heal
Rune   Rado, Wunjo (upright)
Tarot card   The Wheel, The World

Victory

Angel   Perpetiel
Bird (picture or ornament)   eagle
Colour   gold
Colour   red
Creature (picture or ornament)   elephant, goat, leopard, salmon, snail
Crystal   agate, bloodstone
Day   Sunday, Tuesday
Element   fire
Essential oils   carnation, woodruff, benzoin, saffron
God   Thor
Goddess   Freya, Hecate, Morrigan, Themis
Grains   dragon's blood resin
Metal   gold
Planet   Jupiter, Mars, Pluto, Sun
Plants and spices   allspice, beans, bergamot, cedar,
                                       celandine, chamomile, cinnamon,
                                       clove, comfrey, dill, fenugreek,
                                       galangal root, ginger, horse, chestnut,
                                       mandrake, oak, oregano, parsley,

	vervain, vetivert
Rune	Inguz, Sigel, Uruz, Wunjo (upright)
Tarot card	the, six, wands

Visualisation

Angel	Jamaerah, Paschar, Samandiriel
Bird (picture or ornament)falcon	
Colour	black, gold, indigo, violet
Creature (picture or ornament)	butterfly, eagle
Crystal	amber, amethyst, aventurine, blue, lace, agate, celestite, moldavite, clear quartz, smoky quartz
Day	Monday
Element	air
Essential	marjoram, benzoin, myrrh, myrtle
Essential	saffron
God	Odin
Goddess	Cerridwen, Fortuna, Freya, Frigga, Hathor, Hecate
Grains	dragon's blood resin
Metal	copper, silver
Planet	Jupiter, Moon, Neptune, Pluto, Venus
Plants and spices	bluebell, eyebright, marigold, sunflower
Rune	Eihwaz, Peorth (upright)
Tarot card	The Hermit

Wisdom

Angel	Cherubim, Gabriel, Harachel, Manakel, Rehael, Zagzagel
Bird (picture or ornament)	eagle, owl
Colour	indigo, violet
Creature (picture or ornament)	bear, wolf
Crystal	chrysocolla, coral, jade, moldavite, petrified, wood, smoky quartz
Day	Monday

Day	Saturday
Element	earth
Essential, oil	saffron, yarrow, juniper, pine, sandalwood
God	Orion, Lugus, Mimir, Odin
Goddess	Ariadne, Athena, Brigid, Don
Grains	amber, powder, Jerusalem incense
Metal	steel
Planet	Jupiter, Mercury, Saturn, Sun
Plants and spices	beans, borage, cinquefoil, cumin, dill, eyebright, hazelnuts, hyssop, iris, rue, sage, Solomon's seal, thyme, violet
Rune	Tir (upright), Wyrd (no reverse)
Tarot card	The World

Astrological Connection to Tarot Cards

I often use Tarot Cards when I am spell casting and although I have listed them above, here are the court cards which depict the signs of the Zodiac.

Aries	the King Wands
Taurus	the Page of Swords
Gemini	the King Pentacles
Cancer	the King Cups
Leo	the Queen Wands
Virgo	the Queen of Swords
Libra	the King of Swords
Scorpio	the Queen Cups
Sagittarius	the Page Wands
Capricorn	the Page Pentacles
Aquarius	the Queen Pentacles
Pisces	the Page Cups

Meditation

The benefits to be gained from meditation in any of its various forms are many. For the Solitary Witch – for meditation is not a communal act – acquiring the skill of meditation can allow deeper concentration while carrying out rituals and better dedication to any task in hand without the intrusion of the outside world. The energy created from pure concentration from mastering meditation is a powerful thing. It is also a powerful method of aiding worship and giving thanks.

What is Meditation?

The point of all meditation is awareness of self and universe being in total harmony and for Pagans meditation can be a means of casting off mundane thoughts and getting closer to nature and the Deity.

Buddhists aim to eliminate all distractions, become absorbed in thought and move deeper and deeper to acquire an awareness of infinite space.

Kaballistic Jews practise visual meditation, focusing their thoughts on the Tree of Life or the characters of the Jewish alphabet. They also aim to achieve a state of awareness that transcends normal consciousness.

Sufists – the whirling dervishes – achieve a kind of meditative ecstasy by spinning round and round at an ever-increasing rate, hoping to empty the mind of everything apart from communicating with God.

So the aim of meditation for lots of cultures is to create an altered state of consciousness.

Newcomers have no way of knowing how they will respond to it, so it is best to limit the first few sessions to ten minutes at most and not to use it in any ritual until you have mastered it.

Like all things worth doing, the best way to learn meditation is to study with someone who has already mastered it. But till you find that teacher don't be disheartened. Carry on practising basic meditation techniques till you find someone who can help you to get the most out of meditation.

Posture

It is essential to adopt the correct position, not necessarily a sitting one, when meditating. Here are just a few of the simplest positions.

Easy posture

Basically, this involves sitting cross-legged with both feet on the floor. The back should be straight but not tense and the stomach muscles relaxed. With the muscles of the lower back bearing the weight of the body and with the head, neck, and trunk in line, the centre of gravity passes from the base of the spine right through the top of the head. The hands can either be resting lightly on the knees or held in the lap, either one on top of the other or clasped lightly.

Kneeling

Some people find this a convenient and comfortable position for meditation as it is easy to keep the spine straight. Simply kneel on the floor, keeping the knees together. Part the heels and bring the toes together so that you are sitting, straight-backed, on the insides of the feet with the hands on the knees.

Lying flat

Lie flat on the floor on a carpet, blanket, or hard mattress. Part the legs a little and let the feet flop to the side. The arms should be slightly away from the body, hands on the floor, palms up.

Flex each muscle and shake each joint and then relax it before moving on to the next. When you have flexed the face muscles, go back to the beginning and tell each muscle to relax. When you are completely relaxed, lie still for a few minutes simply concentrating on your breathing before starting the meditation proper or assuming one of the other positions.

The Meditation Session

Once you are sitting comfortably, spend a minute or two settling your body and mind, deciding which meditation you will do and how long you will meditate.

Why are you about to meditate? What is your ritual in honour of? What do you hope to achieve by it? The more motivated you are and the clearer your goal, the more successful the meditation is likely to be. The aim of meditation is total involvement of awareness of something.

Proper breathing is vital to proper meditation. Breathe in at your normal rate through the nose. Don't breathe more deeply or more slowly than usual. Remember that to meditate effectively you must be as relaxed as possible.

You could find a meditation object. This is a thing on which the attention can focus and on which it may rest. Make it something relevant and symbolic to your ritual. The object may be something to look at or it may be something you can listen to. Many meditators use a *mantra,* a word or phrase repeated again and again either out loud or mentally.

The meditation object can even be your own breath.

Take up a comfortable posture. You may shut your eyes to aid concentration, but it is better to keep them half open. Breathe as naturally as you can, counting either each inhalation or exhalation up to ten, and repeat this for twenty minutes.

Obstacles

One of the most common obstacles to achieving meditation is a distracted mind. It could be an unresolved problem or worry, or something that has made you angry. Be patient. It takes time and constant practice to learn how to slow down and control the mind. Don't give up.

Another common problem is drowsiness. Meditation can be very relaxing. If you start to feel sleepy while meditating, make sure that you are sitting up straight and your head is not bent too far forward. If you are meditating with your eyes closed, open them and meditate with the gaze directed at the floor just in front of you. If you are meditating in a centrally heated room, turn down the heating or open a window to freshen the air. Increasing the amount of light in the room can also help you to stay awake.

Any physical discomfort makes meditation difficult. Be sure you are comfortable , not too hot or too cold, not too hungry, and that the position you have chosen is one you can hold comfortably for the duration.

Once you have finished meditating, remain in your meditative position for a minute or two and then slowly raise your arms upwards, catlike, quietly reflecting.

When you are finished the meditation or ritual you can drink a glass of water or juice and eat something, preferably something that originates from the earth rather than above the earth. Potatoes, potato scones or potato pancakes will help you to ground yourself. Bread seems like a good idea but it is the seed above the ground that makes the flour rather than the root.

Mantra

Repeating a word or phrase – a mantra – over and over again is probably the oldest ways of mediating. To focus on a mantra during meditation can lead to some of the deepest and most profound sessions you are likely to experience. It creates strong energies.

Sound is energy produced by a vibrating object. It is transmitted by waves of different frequencies. Followers of mantra meditation believe that different sounds resonate with different energy centres in the body and that these sounds can be combined in the form of the mantra.

To practise meditation with a mantra, begin, as usual, by taking up the position that you find most comfortable and breathe gently and rhythmically through the nostrils, taking the breath deep into the abdomen. Then repeat the mantra, either aloud or silently inward, focusing your concentration on it as completely as you can. When your mind has become still, it is no longer necessary to continue repeating the mantra, but, as with other forms of meditation, when you become aware that your thoughts have wandered, start repeating the mantra again, concentrating your conscious thoughts on it.

Chanting

Chanting is a method of creating energy (page 98) and focusing the mind on any particular purpose and the mind provides us with the power of intention. Without the intention it is impossible to create the changes that are required in any form of spell workings.

When spell casting or working in circle for any other purpose, we use simple verses. If we repeat these verses over and over again it becomes a chant and it serves several purposes

1)   You will remain focused on your purpose or intention
2)   You will empower your intention
3)   You will remember the verse for future use

Once you have finished working in your circle you can continue to chant the verse that you are currently using and you can chant your verse while you are walking your dog, washing the dishes, cleaning the house or stuck in a traffic jam. Each time you do this you are empowering your intention and focusing your mind on your goal.

In spellcasting chanting is a very powerful way to raise and release the energy to empower your intention. First create or decide on the words that you will use and then repeat them over and over again getting faster and faster as you do so. Do this until you can't do it any more but do not slow down the pace. Keep the pace going, speaking as fast as you can and then mentally release and stop at the same time. Don't forget to finish with 'An it harm none so mote it be'.

Visual Meditation

Visual meditation uses our natural capacity to think in pictures and our ability to create images in what is often called the mind's eye. It may be practised with the eyes open or shut or by opening and shutting them for alternate periods, concentrating on the after-image that remains in our mind when the eyes are closed. The latter method is most usually recommended for beginners.

Place the object of your meditation at eye level, between a metre and two metres from your face. Assume whichever meditation position you favour, and in as relaxed a way as possible, gaze at the image, focusing your attention on it, trying to become *absorbed* in what you are looking at rather than just thinking about it. After two or three minutes or as soon as you feel any sign of eye strain, close your eyes and visualize the object for as long as you can, still trying to be part of it. Open the eyes again and continue alternating open-eyed and closed-eyed meditation for the full session.

Initially it will be difficult to retain the image in your mind's eye for long when your eyes are closed: don't worry. When the image starts to fade, open the eyes and gaze at the object again. As you become more practised in the art, you will find that you can retain the image for longer and longer.

Meditating on a candle

Many of those who come to visual meditation for the first time find that a lighted candle in a darkened room is the ideal object of focus. Light the candle in a draught-free room so that the flame burns as steadily as possible.

You can dedicate your candle to a spellcasting purpose, carving a symbol into it or coating it in essential oil, for example.

To meditate on the candle, sit as motionless as you can in any of the recommended positions and gaze at the flame so that it holds your attention completely.

Let the image fill your mind for a minute before quickly closing the eyes. Notice how the candle has imprinted itself on the darkness. Hold it in your mind's eye, not worrying about any change of colour. If it slips to the side, bring it back to the centre and keep concentrating until the image fades completely. Now open the eyes and resume gazing at the candle. Continue in this way for ten minutes at first, gradually increasing the time until you can sit comfortably for a full twenty minutes.

Remember if you have dedicated your candle to a spell do not blow it out, but safely allow it to extinguish itself.

The elements
To meditate on any of the elements – air, earth, fire and water – the meditator simply stares at an appropriate object, a pot filled with earth, for example, or a bowl of water.

To visualize any of the four colours – blue, yellow, red and green – simply gaze at an object of that colour—a flower, a piece of fabric, anything at all. To meditate on light, focus the attention on the light cast by a something (like a candle or light bulb). To focus on space you can focus on an empty container.

Symbols, patterns or pictures
Use a symbol of your intention or the protective pentacle as something to meditate on.

Place the symbol so that the central point is at eye level when you are sitting before it in your usual meditating position. Relax the muscles of your face and sit absolutely motionless, gazing at the centre point. Let your gaze move slowly outwards to the edge, taking in but trying not to think about the visual content. Now let the gaze move slowly back to the centre before closing the eyes and holding the image in your mind's eye for as long as you can before opening the eyes again and repeating the process. As you become more practised, you will find that your eye will automatically be drawn to the centre and that it rests there effortlessly on the point that symbolizes the essence of being.

Colour visualizing
There are many methods of using colour as a means of reaching the meditative state. The two given here are among the simplest.

For the first, sit in whichever position you favour and begin to breathe deeply. As usual, don't force the breath, but let it find its own pace and depth. When it has settled to a slow, rhythmic rate, begin to visualize the colours red, orange and yellow, flowing upwards into your solar plexus, visualizing each colour one at a time as a gently flowing river.

Spend a minute or so on each colour and then picture a stream of green flowing into the solar plexus from directly in front of you. After a minute or so, follow the green with blue, indigo and violet, each in turn flowing into you from the same source as the green.

Once the spectrum is completed, imagine yourself bathed in a blue light before ending the meditation by opening your eyes.

Don't be put off if at first you find it difficult to visualize a colour: with practice this becomes easier.

The second method is to sit with eyes closed before focusing the thoughts on any colour you wish. Fill your mind with that colour to the exclusion of everything else and refuse to be frustrated by other thoughts that may come to mind. Wrap them slowly in the colour so that they are enveloped in it. It sometimes helps to imagine an object of your chosen shade—a field of yellow corn perhaps—and gradually concentrate your thoughts on it until the field becomes totally unimportant and your mind is a canvas of yellow. (Some people who practise colour meditation, in fact, begin each session by picturing an easel on which rests a blank canvas that stroke by stroke fills up with the chosen colour.)

Colours for Meditation
Violet

Key word	Purpose
Benefit	Good for meditation and prayer

Indigo

Key word	Sedative
Purpose	Helps to open up our powers of intuition

Blue

Key word	Communication
Purpose	Relaxing and healing

Green

Key word	Balancing
Purpose	Encourages tolerance

Yellow

Key word	Confidence
Purpose	Stimulates mental activity

Orange
    Key word   Creativity
    Purpose   Physically energizing
Red
    Key word   Stimulation
    Purpose   Emotionally energizing
Magenta
    Key word   Balancing
    Purpose   Achieving fulfilment
Turquoise
    Key word   Peace
    Purpose   To improve the nervous and immune system
Pink
    Key word   Loving
    Purpose   Encourages unconditional love
Black
    Key word   Space
    Purpose   Spirituality and meditation
White
    Key word   Illumination
    Purpose   Achieving clarity of thought

Tactile Meditation

Before you begin, choose an object to hold while you are meditating – something light, for if it is too heavy its weight will affect your concentration and hence your focus. It should not be sharp. Now close your eyes and concentrate on the texture of the object in your hand.

Another method of using touch to help reach the meditative state requires either a set of worry beads or four or five pebbles. Relax in your favourite position, holding the beads or pebbles in the open palm of one hand and with the other move them rhythmically and methodically between your fingers, counting them one at a time.

Feel each pebble as you count, focusing all your attention on the slow, repetitive movement.

Music and Meditation

The relevance of music as an aid to meditation is a personal one. Its effect on you depends on your own instincts and intuitions.

Percussion instruments have long been used in meditation. The music they produce symbolises rhythm and vitality. Gongs and bells are said to purify the surrounding atmosphere making it more conducive to meditation.

The gentle tinkling of the Aeolian harp can create a perfectly calm state of mind as you approach your meditations, and help you to focus your thought.

To meditate to music, take up your usual position, close your eyes and listen to a significant piece, immersing yourself in it completely. Try to become one with the sound, letting it encompass you. If your thoughts are invaded by memories associated with the piece you have selected, imagine them as musical notes floating off into the distance.

Once you have learned to meditate, it is a skill that you will have for the rest of your life, but while it will give you a sense of inner serenity it does not mean that you are free of pressures and disturbing emotions. Meditation is not an escape from these problems: it enables you to see them as something you can deal with.

Once you have become used to meditation, you will find you can practise it anywhere – on a train, in an aeroplane, at your office desk during the course of a working day.

And remember there is no right way to meditate and no wrong way to meditate. The only right way is the one that you are most comfortable with, the one that enables you to get out of meditation whatever it is you want.

Ingredients for Meditation Rituals

Meditation and astral travel
Sandalwood, mugwort, and cinnamon lavender.

Passion
Sandalwood, rose, galangal, periwinkle.

Peace
Lemon, rose, lilac.

Prosperity
Cinnamon, vervain, ginger, orange peel, sandalwood, galangal, nasturtium seeds frankincense, heliotrope, tonka, cedar, patchouli, galangal, ginger, allspice, patchouli, myrrh, cinnamon, sandalwood, orris, pine, basil.

Protection from a stalker
Chili powder, asafoetida pepper, orris, sage, tobacco ashes, nutmeg, cinnamon.

Protection, general
Angelica, ash leaves, barley, basil, betony, burdock, chamomile, chili pepper, dragon's blood, ivy, mustard seed, turmeric, galangal, rosemary, orris, sandalwood, salt, vetivert, vervain, galangal, peppermint, rue, cinnamon, mugwort, dill, juniper, frankincense, cumin.

Purification
Bay, betony, basil, chili pepper, cumin, dragon's blood, horseradish, loosestrife, mint, nettle, sandalwood, wintergreen galangal, nasturtium seeds, patchouli.

Sobriety
Orris root, sweet flag oil.

Spirituality
Jasmine, violet, lavender frankincense, sandalwood, myrrh.

Strength
Basil, rum, bay, thyme, aloe.

Success
Sandalwood, orris, allspice, musk mint, rose, nutmeg.

Knot Magick

Contributed by Anna Franklin

One of the first things that we encounter in life is a knot, when the midwife cuts and knots the umbilical cord. In times past, this was a magickal act when she could bestow a good or bad fate on the child. Throughout history, the tying of the knot is associated with the binding of a spell, while the untying of a knot represents releasing magick or breaking enchantment. Knots were used to contain illness, secure love, confine evil spirits, weave blessings, control the weather, and bind curses.

Some of the magickal implications of knot magick still survive in the English language where people speak of marriage as 'tying the knot', or in other words the couple are bound together. In certain marriage customs of some parts of the world, the couple's hands are actually tied together to symbolise this, just as they are in the Pagan ceremony of handfasting. Then again, when we part from someone, we may speak of 'severing the bond'.

The use of knots for magick is very old, known throughout the ancient world. The Egyptians used knots for many magickal purposes, symbolising the controlling and releasing of both creative and destructive forces. For example, the seven Hathors [fairy Godmother figures] were invoked to bless a new born child with seven knots tied in a cloth, while incantations were chanted over them. In ancient Egypt, the knot was a symbol of Isis, usually depicted as a knotted cloth between her breasts. This knot was represented in an amulet called a *tyet*, sometimes referred to as the girdle or buckle of Isis, or sometimes as the blood of Isis. Some scholars have suggested that this knot represented her 'sacred blood' or menstrual blood, or in other words, referring to her role as mother and fertility Goddess. According to the 186th chapter of the Book of the Dead The blood of Isis, the virtue of Isis, the magick power of Isis, the magick power of the Eye, are protecting this the Great One; they prevent any wrong being done to him.

The knot was also a sacred emblem of the Goddess Inanna, and was the first written form of her name. As a symbol of authority it appeared on the top of a tall pole, a symbol that developed into the later crosier, carried by Christian bishops.

When the knot is tied, it is considered to be binding something up, or tying in the magick. When it is untied, it is considered to be releasing something, or releasing the magick. An ancient Mesopotamian magician might curse someone by reciting the curse while tying knots in a cord, which would then be buried to keep the curse in place. A disease might be cured by tying thread around an afflicted person's limbs, while the magician transferred the illness into the thread by a spell. The cord was then cut off and thrown away, taking the disease with it.

In many societies, women about to give birth would make sure that all knots in clothing and furnishings were untied so that the baby would slip easily from the womb. Jews forbade the tying of knots on the Sabbath in case they should constrict male potency. In a similar vein, Rome's high priest, the Flamen Dialis, was not allowed to wear any knot on his person, for fear 'restricting' his power. Early Muslims offered prayers to Allah to be protected from all those who blow on knots [to imbue them with magickal life]. There are several Greek myths that speak of a hero being given a bag in which the winds are bound, and to release them he must untie the string that secures it. As untying something releases it, tying up binds it, so sympathetic magick to stop the flow of blood from wounds might consist of tying knots in a piece of cord.

More recently, English witches were believed to be able to tie up the winds by knotting strings, which would then be sold to sailors to provide good weather for sailing. However, they were also suspected of using knot magick to also inflict illness and disability by closing eyes, mouths, or throats, or by restricting the movements of limbs with knot magick.

The whole idea of magick being concerned with knots, spinning or weaving comes from the powerful idea that a web of energy connects everything. It is often thought of as being spun by a creator God or Goddess. In Welsh legend, the weaver is Arianrhod, mistress of Caer Arianrhod, the Spiral Castle of death, initiation, and rebirth. Out of her own body she spins the thread of being, and weaves it to form matter the cosmos itself. She is lady of fate who spins the thread of destiny and weaves the web that joins all life together. Her spinning wheel is the wheel of the stars, her threads the threads of life, death, and rebirth. Her castle reflects the spiralling thread. The ancients saw it as the Corona Borealis at the North Star, where souls regenerated.

According to Greek myth the three Fates or Moerae control human destiny. The thread of life is spun on Clotho's spindle, measured by the rod of Lachesis, and snipped by Atropos' shears. In stature, Atropos was the smallest of the three, but by far the most feared, relating as she does to the hag of winter, the death Goddess 'she who cannot be stayed'. Prayers and

please would not move them and even the Gods could not alter the decrees
of the Fates.

The Latin word *fatum* or fate referred to a pronouncement of destiny, a
spoken sentence of doom fixed by the Gods at birth. Shakespeare speaks
of them as 'the Wyrde Systres' [Macbeth], a term derived from the Anglo
Saxon *wyrd*, meaning fate, destiny, or the power that controls them. Wyrd
Sisters is a term applied to the Norns, another trio of fate Goddesses. It
is possible that The Fates were the original fairy Godmothers; they were
believed to assist at the birth of certain [if not all] humans. Long after the
coming of Christianity, mothers would make ready for them when a baby
was due, spreading out food and gifts to ensure their favour for the child.
Just as the fairies were called 'good people' in supplication, the Fates were
titled *Parcae*, or 'merciful'. Belief in them survived in parts of Greece well
into the twentieth century.

The word 'fairy' is probably derived from the Latin for fate *fata*, via the
Old French *fée*. Large numbers of fairies are associated with spinning, either
spinning themselves or maliciously destroying the spinning of others. Some
of these fairies are traceable to ancient spinning and weaving Goddesses,
who spin the thread of the cosmos and weave the web of fate. Several fairies
are said to destroy any spinning left on the wheel at Yule or Christmas.
This has its origin in the fact that many sun Gods and Goddesses span
the cosmos or the sunbeams in the hours before dawn. At Yule ['Wheel'],
the midwinter solstice, when the sun stands still, all forms of spinning and
weaving were forbidden. The Lapps forbade the turning of any kind of
wheel, including cartwheels and churns.

The concept of a uniting field of energy as a web, net or woven
cloth is widespread in India it is called Tantra, meaning 'web' or 'fabric' or it
is called the 'jewelled net of Indra'. In South America it was called 'the net
of power'. Here in Britain it was called the Web of Wyrd. The Old English
word *wyrd* is derived from the verb *weorðan*, which means 'to become', or
'to come to pass'. This web is constantly being woven by events, actions, and
thoughts. Manipulating it – moving, binding, or tying its threads –is an act
of magick.

The web binds everything together – nothing is separate.
Everything we can see, such as people, rocks, plants and animals, and the all
things we can't see, including the Gods, are woven together as a single whole.
This is implicate in the occult principle of 'as above, so below'. All aspects
of the Cosmos are reflections of 'one thing' which underlies and connects
them. What happens in the greater Cosmos is reflected here in the physical

realm; events on Earth run parallel to events in the greater Cosmos because both are part of the One. This is the basis of such arts as astrology and divination, where the warp and weft of the greater pattern are discerned within specific threads such as the movement of the planets, the flight of a raven, or the fall of a tarot card. It follows that what affects a small part of the Cosmos eventually affects the whole in some way. By manipulating events below in specific and powerful ways, using consciousness and intent, the greater pattern will be affected - and this is the basis of magick. Every thought, every action has consequences that shape the web and become our collective reality.

In witchcraft we use weaving and knotting as conscious acts of magick to affect the web. In ritual, we weave together the disparate threads of time, place and people using the beliefs, words, symbols, movements and intent of those involved to make the ritual pattern, a pattern by which we establish a link between us and the greater whole. Ritual is a two way exchange between the microcosm (us and through us, our world) and the macrocosm (the greater Cosmos and the powers of the Gods).

At initiation, a modern witch consecrates his or her magickal cord, which is usually nine feet long and worn about the waist. The neophyte is asked to fashion the cord themselves, plaiting it from new wool over many weeks or months, weaving enchantment into it. This cord is then used to measure the circumference of the magick circle, and for knot magick, either solo or in company with other members of the coven. Sometimes covens keep a set of cords in various colours for group spells.

The simplest form of knot magick is to tie nine knots in a cord, alternating them from each end and working towards the centre, concentrating on what it is you wish to achieve, then releasing it into the knot. There are several variations on the accompanying chant:

By the knot of one, the spell's begun
By the knot of two, my wish come true
By the knot of three, the magick's free
By the knot of four, my will be law
By the knot of five, the spell will thrive
By the knot of six, the magick fix
By the knot of seven, my words to heaven
By the knot of eight, the magick create
By the knot of nine, this thing be mine.

Put the cord somewhere safe and leave it as long as you wish the spell to work. When you wish to undo the spell, undo or cut the knots.

One of the best-known uses of knot magick is in the witch's ladder. For this a length of cord is tied with a certain number of knots, some say thirteen, others say forty. The ladder is then used like a Catholic rosary to keep track of chants, or during meditation, with the knots counted between finger and thumb, and the spell or magickal intent being re-affirmed with each knot counted. This is actually a modern version of the original witch's ladder which had a much darker purpose and was used to bind an enemy, tying some of his or her hair into the knots.

You don't have to use a heavy cord for magick, but could use a thread or ribbon. It doesn't have to be nine feet long either, but does work best if the measurement is in some multiple of three – three inches, three feet, six inches, six feet, nine inches, nine feet [or nine centimetres for that matter] and so on.

You might use different numbers of knots for different purposes, according to the laws of numerology

One	–	unity, wholeness, healing, Sun magick
Two	–	duality, choice, the emotions, Moon magick
Three	–	creativity, production, action, Mars magick
Four	–	material matters, foundation, wealth, communication, Mercury magick
Five	–	expansion, growth, joyfulness, Jupiter magick
Six	–	love, beauty, harmony, Venus magick
Seven	–	limitation, ending, binding, Saturn magick
Eight	–	dissolution, endings and beginnings, balance, Pluto magick
Nine	–	three times three, the number of the Goddess, the number of truth and the meeting of all three planes of existence

You can enhance the magick by using a thread or ribbon of the appropriate colour

Red	–	life, vitality, health
Pink	–	love
Blue	–	healing, peace, spirituality
Black	–	endings, negation of ego
Green	–	growth, creativity, wealth
Orange	–	optimism, joy

Yellow   –   thought, mental activity
Purple   –   power, assertion, confidence
White   –   spirituality, protection

Use a little imagination, and the uses of knot magick are unlimited. For example, to bring two people together, use two threads in different colours to represent them. Loosely knot the two threads together, and then pull them tight. To protect a vulnerable person, you could obtain something that belongs to them, a button or earring perhaps, and tie it in a protective basket of knots. You might use threads of differing colours to weave in various strands of magick; green for growth, orange for joy, pink for new love and so on. Tie in beads to bring in extra elements of colour magick, feathers to represent messages and the element of air, and gemstones according to their correspondences– amethyst for healing, rose quartz for peace, and so on. Do a little research into the tying of knots, and use different types of knots for different purposes. Remember that knotting, weaving and braiding symbolises the bringing together of disparate elements, and binding them together.

Candle Magick

Candle Magick is another way to empower your ritual or spell and it is simple to perform. You will need a candle of the appropriate colour and some essential oil or a blend of oils to anoint the candle.

A circle is cast in the standard way then taking your boline or something with a sharp point, and candle begin to inscribe symbols appropriate for your spell or ritual. Inscribe these symbols at the top of your candle rather than at the bottom otherwise you will have to wait through the entire burning process for your spell or ritual to become empowered.

Once you have inscribed your symbols put the candle down and then place a little of your chosen oil in the palm of your hand then with the palms of your hands flat, in the prayer position, rub them together briskly until they become very warm. As you do so, focus all your energy and intention on the space between your hands. Continue this until you have mentally empowered and visualised your intention and uttered the words to convey your desire. Now pick up your inscribed candle and anoint it from middle to top with the oil. Repeat this several times until the candle is covered in the oil all round the top then anoint it from middle to the bottom again repeating several times until the candle is fully coated with a thin film of anointed oil. Place it in the candle holder and light is saying 'And it harm none so mote it be'.

If you have to put a spell candle out DO NOT BLOW IT OUT wet your fingers and pinch it out or use a candle snuff.

Components for Candle Spells

Answers Candle Spell

Day of the week	Wednesday
Time of day	5am, Noon, 7pm or at any time in the evening when the moon is waxing or full but not when it is waning
Goddess	Themis
God	Woden
Planet	Mercury
Star Sign	Gemini or Virgo

Metal	Quicksilver
Colour	Orange, yellow or green
Rune	Ansuz
Symbol	Books or calculators
Number	9
Crystal	opal, aquamarine, hematite, jet
Flower	Lavender
Herb	Angelica
Essential oil	Marjoram
Tree	Oak

Career Candle Spell

Day of the week	Sunday
Time of day	5am, Noon, 7pm or at any time in the evening when the moon is waxing or full but not when it is waning
Goddess	Oshion and the God Re, the power of the Sun
Guardian Angel	Michael
Star Sign	Leo
Metal	Gold
Colour	Yellow, orange
Rune	Tir
Symbol	Keys
Number	5
Crystal	Citrine, tiger's eye, sunstone
Flower	Marigold
Herb	Chamomile
Tree	Hazel
Essential oil	Bergamot

Communication Candle Spell

Day of the week	Wednesday
Time of day	5am, Noon, 7pm or at any time in the evening when the moon is waxing or full but not when it is waning
Goddess	Shakti
God	Amotken
Planet	Mercury

Guardian Angel	Raphael
Star Sign	Scorpio
Metal	silver
Colour	green
Rune	Ansuz
Symbol	Writing materials
Number	6
Crystal	Malachite
Flower	White lotus or chrysanthemum
Essential oil	Geranium
Herb	Parsley
Tree	Rowan

Courage Candle Spell

Day of the week	Tuesday
Time of day	5am, Noon, 7pm or at any time in the evening when the moon is waxing or full but not when it is waning
Goddess	Lillith
God	Bes
Planet	Mars
Guardian Angel	Samael
Star Sign	Aries
Metal	Iron
Colour	Red
Rune	Tiewaz
Symbol	Sword
Number	4
Crystal	Jade, bloodstone or malachite
Flower	Honeysuckle
Essential oil	Lavender
Herb	Pepper
Tree	Holly

Fertility Candle Spell

Goddess	Venus
God	Min
Planet	Mars or Venus
Guardian Angel	Raziel

Star Sign	Scorpio
Metal	Iron
Colour	Red
Rune	Beork
Symbol	Eggs
Number	1,3
Crystal	Moonstone, carnelian
Flower	Hyacinth
Essential oil	Frankincense
Herb	Mint
Tree	Birch

Forgiveness Candle Spell

Day of the week	Wednesday
Time of day	5am, Noon, 7pm or at any time in the evening when the moon is waxing or full but not when it is waning
Goddess	Hera
God	Zeus
Planet	Neptune
Guardian Angel	Sabbathi
Star Sign	Pisces
Metal	Platinum
Colour	Violet
Rune Symbol	Eolh
Number	6
Crystal	Apache teardrop (obsidian)
Flower	Daffodil
Essential oil	Cedarwood
Herb	Angelica
Tree	Ash

Friendship Candle Spell

Day of the week	Monday
Time of day	5am, Noon, 7pm or at any time in the evening when the moon is waxing or full but not when it is waning
Goddess	Luna
God	Horus

Planet	Moon
Guardian Angel	Gabriel
Star Sign	Cancer
Metal	Silver
Colour	White, silver, orange, yellow
Rune	Gefu
Symbol	Pairs of things
Number	Any even number, 2,4,6,8,…
Crystal	Moonstone
Flower	Freesia
Essential oil	Patchouli
Tree	Silver birch
Herb	Fennel

Good Luck Candle Spell

Day of the week	Thursday
Time of day	5am, Noon, 7pm or at any time in the evening when the moon is waxing or full but not when it is waning
Goddess	Gamelia
God	Quirinus
Planet	Jupiter
Guardian Angel	Zadkiel
Star Sign	Sagittarius
Metal	Tin, silver, gold
Colour	Blue
Rune	Dagaz
Symbol	Two-sided objects such as coins. Your birth number calculated by adding together the day, month and year of your birth.
Crystal	Citrine or amber
Flower	White heather
Essential oil	Sandalwood
Herb	Clover
Tree	Cedar

Gratitude Candle Spell

Day of the week	Monday

Time of day	5am, Noon, 7pm or at any time in the evening when the moon is waxing or full but not when it is waning
Goddess	Rangda
God	Telephos
Planet	Moon
Guardian Angel	Gabriel
Star Sign	Pisces
Metal	Silver
Colour	White
Rune	Kano
Symbol	Circular objects and fruit
Number	3
Crystal	Snow quartz or opal
Flower	Hibiscus
Essential oil	Bergamot
Herb	Saffron
Tree	Birch

Harvest Candle Spell

Day of the week	Saturday
Time of day	5am, Noon, 7pm or at any time in the evening when the moon is waxing or full but not when it is waning
Goddess	Ceres
God	Apis
Planet	Saturn
Star Sign	Capricorn
Metal	Lead
Colour	Deep blue
Rune	Jera
Symbol	Autumn leaves, wheat sheaves, grains or breads
Number	9
Crystal	Lapis or amber
Flower	Violet
Essential oil	Sage
Tree	Bamboo

Health Candle Spell

Day of the week	Sunday
Time of day	5am, Noon, 7pm or at any time in the evening when the moon is waxing or full but not when it is waning
Goddess	Brigit
God	Hapy
Planet	Neptune
Guardian Angel	Germaine
Star Sign	Pisces
Metal	Gold
Colour	Green, yellow or violet
Rune	Beork
Symbol	Fish
Number	3
Crystal	Clear quartz
Flower	Marigold, daffodil or sunflower
Essential oil	Sandalwood
Herb	Lavender
Tree	Ash

Home Candle Spell

Day of the week	Monday
Time of day	5am, Noon, 7pm or at any time in the evening when the moon is waxing or full but not when it is waning
Goddess	Heket
God	Dagda
Planet	The Moon
Guardian Angel	Haniel
Star Sign	Cancer or Taurus
Metal	Silver or gold
Colour	Green, gold or silver
Rune	Othel
Symbol	Hand knitted or sewn items, cakes, breads
Number	4
Crystal	Rhodocrosite

Flower	Honeysuckle
Essential Oil	Jasmine
Tree	Rowan
Herb	Myrrh

Inspiritation Candle Spell

Day of the week	Saturday
Time of day	5am, Noon, 7pm or at any time in the evening when the moon is waxing or full but not when it is waning
Goddess	Ostara
God	Telesphoros
Planet	Uranus
Guardian Angel	Arvath
Star Sign	Aquarius
Metal	Aluminium
Colour	Indigo
Rune	Ansuz
Symbol	Key
Number	1
Crystal	Amethyst
Flower	Anemones
Essential oil	Peppermint
Herb	Sage
Tree	Hazel

Interviews Candle Spell

Day of the week	Wednesday
Time of day	5am, Noon, 7pm or at any time in the evening when the moon is waxing or full but not when it is waning
Goddess	Kali
God	Kaineus
Guardian Angel	Raphael
Planet	Mercury
Star Sign	Gemini or Virgo
Metal	Quicksilver
Colour	Slver or indigo
Rune	Wunjo

Symbol	Papers certificates or official documents
Number	4, 5, 7,
Crystal	Amethyst Tigers eye
Flower	Almond blossom
Herb	Dill
Essential oil	Lemongrass
Tree	Hazel

Love Candle Spell

Day of the week	Friday
Time of day	5am, Noon, 7pm or at any time in the evening when the moon is waxing or full but not when it is waning
Goddess	Freya
God	Osiris
Planet	Venus
Guardian Angel	Arnad
Star Sign	Taurus
Metal	Copper or brass
Colour	Pink, red or orange
Rune	Inguz
Symbol	Hearts
Number	2
Crystal	Rose quartz, emerald or sapphire.
Flower	Lavender, lilac, red rose or jasmine
Essential oil	Rose bulgar, rose maroc, ylang ylang, geranium, jasmine
Herb	Rose
Tree	Apple

Marriage Candle Spell

Day of the week	Friday
Time of day	5am, Noon, 7pm or at any time in the evening when the moon is waxing or full but not when it is waning
Goddess	Freya
God	Khnum
Planet	Venus

Guardian Angel	Adonai
Star Sign	Taurus Libra
Metal	Rose, gold, copper
Colour	Red, pink or green
Rune	Gefu, Ingux, Manaz
Symbol	Rings
Number	2, 4, 6
Crystal	Rose quartz
Flower	Rose
Essential oil	Rose otto
Tree	Apple
Herb	Ylang Ylang

Opportunities Candle Spell

Day of the week	Sunday
Time of day	5am, Noon, 7pm or at any time in the evening when the moon is waxing or full but not when it is waning
Goddess	Carna
God	Khonsu
Planet	Sun
Star Sign	Leo
Metal	Gold
Colour	Yellow
Rune	Kano, Dagaz
Symbol	keys doors
Number	7
Crystal	Diamond, ruby, sunstone or citrine
Flower	Jasmine
Essential oil	Neroli
Tree	Cherry

Passion Candle Spell

Day of the week	Tuesday
Time of day	5am, Noon, 7pm or at any time in the evening when the moon is waxing or full but not when it is waning
Goddess	Lillith
God	Narcissus

Planet	Venus
Guardian Angel	Gamelie
Star Sign	Scorpio, Taurus, Libra
Metal	Copper and brass
Colour	Red, orange, green
Rune	Ingux
Symbol	Fire
Number	1
Crystal	Emerald and sapphire
Flower	Poppy and tiger lily
Essential oil	Patchouli
Tree	Pine
Herb	Fennel

Peace Candle Spell

Day of the week	Friday
Time of day	5am, Noon, 7pm or at any time in the evening when the moon is waxing or full but not when it is waning
Goddess	Pax
God	Odysseus
Planet	Venus
Guardian Angel	Arnad
Star Sign	Taurus
Metal	Copper or rose gold
Colour	White
Rune	Othel
Symbol	Cone shaped items
Number	2
Crystal	Rhodochrosite
Flower	White lily
Essential oil	Marjoram
Herb	Chamomile
Tree	Olive

Prosperity Candle Spell

Day of the week	Sunday
Time of day	5am, Noon, 7pm or at any time in the evening when the moon is waxing or

	full but not when it is waning
Goddess	Aditi
God	Pallas, Athene
Planet	Sun
Guardian Angel	Michael
Star Sign	Leo
Metal	Gold
Colour	Yellow
Rune	Fehu
Symbol	Coal, salt, money or keys
Number	9
Crystal	Diamond, jade or ruby
Flower	Sunflower
Essential oil	Rose otto
Herb	Bay
Tree	Cherry

Protection Candle Spell

Day of the week	Thursday
Time of day	5am, Noon, 7pm or at any time in the evening when the moon is waxing or full but not when it is waning
Goddess	Callisto
God	Thor
Planet	Jupiter
Guardian Angel	Zadkiel
Star Sign	Sagittarius
Metal	Tin
Colour	Blue
Rune	Eohl
Symbol	Ankh
Number	8
Crystal	Turquoise
Flower	Lilac and apple blossom
Essential oil	Frankincense
Herb	Garlic, mint or feverfew
Tree	Rowan

Secrets Candle Spell

Day of the week	Wednesday
Time of day	5am, Noon, 7pm or at any time in the evening when the moon is waxing or full but not when it is waning
Goddess	Cybelle
God	Tiw
Planet	Sun, Mars
Guardian Angel	Jesodoth
Star Sign	Aries or Scorpio
Metal	Iron
Colour	Yellow, red, green or blue
Rune	Jara
Symbol	Money
Number	9
Crystal	Bloodstone, flint, malachite, jade
Flower	marigold or chamomile
Herb	Fennel
Essential oil	Rosemary or bergamot.
Tree	Laurel

Success Candle Spell

Day of the week	Wednesday
Time of day	5am, Noon, 7pm or at any time in the evening when the moon is waxing or full but not when it is waning
Goddess	Cybelle
God	Tiw
Planet	Sun, Mars
Guardian	Angel Jesodoth
Star Sign	Aries or Scorpio
Metal	Iron
Colour	Yellow, red, green or blue
Rune	Jara
Symbol	money
Number	9
Crystal	Bloodstone, flint, malachite, jade,
Flower	marigold or chamomile

Herb	Fennel
Essential oil	Rosemary or bergamot.
Tree	Laurel

Travel Candle Spell

Day of the week	Tuesday
Time of day	5am, Noon, 7pm or at any time in the evening when the moon is waxing or full but not when it is waning
Goddess	Dag
God	Geb
Planet	Uranus
Guardian Angel	Michael
Star Sign	Sagittarius
Metal	Radium
Colour	Pale Blue
Rune	Rad
Symbol	Passports tickets, maps, wheels, or spheres
Number	19
Crystal	Turquoise, chrysolite
Flower	Yellow Daisy
Essential oil	Basil
Herb	Caraway
Tree	Oak

Victory Candle Spell

Day of the week	Tuesday
Time of day	5am, Noon, 7pm or at any time in the evening when the moon is waxing or full but not when it is waning
Goddess	Athena
God	Khepri
Planet	Mars
Guardian Angel	Soltaan
Star Sign	Aries
Metal	Iron or Steel
Colour	Red
Rune	Sigel

Symbol	Medals
Number	1
Crystal	Bloodstone
Flower	Marguerite or daisy
Essential oil	Pine
Herb	Tarragon
Tree	Hawthorn

Ritual Verses

Banishing Ritual Verse

Problems in the past I had,
So many did I know,
But now I bury all the bad
And ask my seeds to grow.
And as they grow they feed upon
That which I do not want.
My problems now they will be gone
As seed becomes a plant.
Grow for me, and flower too,
My problems now are gone.
This coming year will be so good
As problems I have none.
An it harm none so mote it be.

Beltane Verse

We jump the fire and celebrate love,
We jump the fire and celebrate life.
This fertile land will bring us fruits,
This cleansing fire ends winter's strife

Blessing Ritual Verse

May every blessing you bestow
Return to you, but three times more.
The Lady watches and she knows,
Blessings she gives and love she shows.
So mote it be.

Birthday Ritual Verse

I ask the Goddess up above

Bless our ******* with lots of love
She is shining true and pure
Her love for you is steady and sure.

Grant *******'s wishes on this day
Bring him/her joy in work and play.
Good news from friends both far and near
Let there be music for all to hear.

Break a Curse Ritual Verse

I break the curse that came to me,
That I be well for all to see.
I send it back form whence it came
The bidder takes back all the pain.

I am free from any outfall,
Free to live and love to all,
The three-fold rule the Goddess gave
For her children, them to save.

We bide this rule and do no harm
The curse returned and sender warned.
Be mindful of what ere you send
It will come back and you will bend.
And it harm none so mote it be

Break a Spell Ritual Verse

A spell I made without good thought
The consequences of.
I ask that it should come to naught
Assistance from above.
Lord and Lady hear my plea
An harm none so mote it be.

Business Ritual Verse

This work I do I ere do well
And often do succeed
But here and now I ask the Lord
My business should sprout seed.
My plans to grow and bear good fruit
Just like the Lady doth
I give my word I will work hard
Of this I give my oath
An it harm none so mote it be

Casting a Circle Ritual Verse

This circle line I now prepare
Let no one enter should they dare
This sacred space I dedicate
Filled with love and never hate
So mote it be

Cleaning a Circle Ritual Verse

I sweep, I sweep my circle clean
Out with the dirt and out with the mean.
The energy now is pure and sweet
My circle now is clean and neat.

Creative Writing Ritual Verse

From the Goddess up above
May she bless you with light and love.
May your pen write straight and true
With wisdom, insight and knowledge too.
Share with those who think they know,
Give guidance so that they may follow.
She who radiates the page you write,
Blesses you with love and insight
And it harm none so mote it be.

Divination Ritual Verse 1

Crystals pure and oh so bright
Bless me now with your insight
Show me now what I should know
Lead me now and I will follow
So mote it be.

Divination Ritual Verse 2

Lady and Lord this day is long
As night approaches I worship thee
I work and play and sing my song
I sing my song my prayer to thee
I ask of you to grant to me
Wishes one and two and three
My worship is both true and pure
My thanks I offer to be sure

Let me see what lies ahead. To be hopeful, never dread
Let me see the mystery. Understanding grant to me
Let me know the truth unfold
My words then doth Wisdom hold
Repeat

Drawing Down the Moon Ritual Verse

Luna, Lady high above
Come bless me now
With light and love
Hear my prayer at full of moon
Come now, come soon.
She who lives within our kind
Bless our body heart and mind
Welcome here into my space
Let me gaze upon your face
Lady I have known your name
Yet your purpose stays the same

Mother Maiden Goddess true
Empower me now to feel anew
Feel the love I give to you
Feel my worship pure and true
This I promise on this night
You are all my love my light
Keep me safe and free from harm
Bless me now with all your charm
I have known you many times
May I know you many more
Let me be as one with you
I am she who gives all life
On this blessed Esbat night
I am she this full moon night

Friendship Ritual Verse

Our friends may come and they may go
But always they will be
Close to my heart and in my thoughts
Wherever they may be

They have no doubts they always know
Our love doth cross o'er land and see
Our friendship travels where they go
And lasts eternally

Hear my spell I ask of you
My Lady from above
Success to them in all they do
And blessed with light and love

Goddess Ritual Verse

I sing to the Goddess I sing blessed be
I invoke the Goddess by the power of three
The maiden the mother the old crone I call
I worship and honour her one and all

Harvest Ritual Verse

Thanks we give for all received
From seeds that we have sown
We watched our crops in fields of green
And blessed with what we've grown

Soon winter comes and we grow cold
Though fires are burning brightly
We tend the frail we tend the old
We keep our vigil nightly

We here do ask our stocks and stores
Our flour for bread our harvest too
May they keep till springtime comes
And last the winter through.

Healing Ritual Verse

I ask for healing from above
To bless **** with light and love
Bring good health this is my plea
So she/he be well for all to see

Imbolc (Candlemas Verse)

I light these candles to clean and to heal.
Let flame light my purpose – let candle reveal
The good work I've done – and the work that remains.
I give thanks for our house and for all it contains.
Let body and mind and home be cleansed.
An it harm none so be it.

Lammas Verse

We bake our bread, give thanks and pray,
For the Lammas crops we reap this day.

The Sun God's gifts from fertile earth,
For these good fruits we show our worth.
Oh Mother Earth be fruitful still,
Let future crops our larders fill.
We meet in love and gratitude
For Summer's harvest of good food

Legal Ritual Verse

Legal battle to fight and win
Justice aid us see their sin
Victory be ours to see
So that all of us be free
Free from anger free from strife
Free from interference rife
Lessons they are meant to learn
Help us please great Lord Herne

Litha Verse

Each day that comes, my strength doth grow.
Oh Lord and Lady I've come to know,
You hear my prayers and answer me,
Your love and bounty sets me free.
This Litha day your power and grace
They purify and bless this place.
Accept these gifts I leave for you,
My love, as ever, always true.

Love Ritual Verse

My heart is empty no one to love
Lady bless me from above
Let me love me then love I give
Show me love and how to live
Peace Ritual Verse
Let peace be felt upon the land
No weapons lifted by any hand

May farmers prosper
As animals graze
And Pax be with us
To hear our praise.

Mabon Verse

For our blessings we thank the Goddess
And think on those who have much less.
No food on their table, no bed to rest in
No roof to shelter them from rain,
Good health and happiness, good people around them,
No-one and nothing to ease their pain.
Let us give to those in need,
With heart and pocket and thought and deed.

Ostara (Easter) Verse

I plant my seed that it may grow,
My hopes within it, too, I sow.
Dear Goddess see what I pursue,
And help me see my dreams come true.
If I deserve it through work and toil –
Here symbolised by fertile soil –
The day will come, through my volition,
When I will see my work's fruition.
An it harm none, do what thou will.

Prosperity Ritual Verse

Blessed Lady of the Light
Fill my purse this is my plight
Bills to pay and food to buy
Hear my prayer hear my cry

Protection Verse

Enfold us in your warm embrace
Safe from harm we be
Protect us now and for always
It is our wish, so mote it be.

Property Moving Verse

With fire and light I bring to life
Intentions honest, free from strife
I ask The Lady, Hear my plea
Grant my wishes, set me free
By candle light I make my vow
The time for us to move is now
No more delays to circumvent
With funds secured we're all content
A home filled with joy and peace
Blessed with love above and beneath
It is our will for all to see
An it harm none so mote it be!

Purification Ritual Verse

Salt is life here is life
Sacred be without strife,
Salt is life here is life
Sacred be without strife,
Salt is life here is life
Blessed be without strife.

Purification Ritual Verse for tools

Bless it clean bless it pure
Make its purpose true & sure
Vibrations dark do send away
Keep Pure & light from this day

Recalling Dreams Ritual Verse

A dream a dream I had last night
But now I can't recall
I dedicate this crystal light
To tell me tell me all

Samhain Verse

Enfold us in your loving embrace
And keep us safe from harm.
Wherever we are, whatever place,
Keep us fed and warm.
The old ones who have gone before, return to grace our table,
Welcome say we, one and all, return if you are able.
Guide us, teach us, show us how to walk the sacred way,
That we may teach the ones who follow by the words we say

Spirit Guidance Ritual Verse

For wise ones elders to come to me
The open door allows them entry
Angels, Loved Ones guide us now
If they can pass the guardian sentry
Now's the time that we do bow
To the wisdom from above
Teach us show us what we should know
That comes to us with light and love

Success Ritual Verse

Success may come and it may go
The wheel doth ever turn
But what we do and what we know
Work hard and we will earn

For efforts made rewards we reap

The Lady blesses those
She grant to us, our bounty keep
Her love to us she shows

Yule Verse

Old friendships renewed, and loved ones return,
Good feelings imbued, as our fires they burn,
Our future as bright, as the Lady's light.
The Sun God is born, and our hearths are warm,
With loved ones we share our love and our fayre.

The Witches' Chant

by Doreen Valiente

Darksome night and shining Moon,
Hell's dark mistress Heaven's Queen
Harken to the Witches' rune,
Diana, Lilith, Melusine!
Queen of witchdom and of night,
Work my will by magic rite.
Earth and water, air and fire,
Conjured by the witch's blade,
Move you unto my desire,
Aid ye as the charm is made!
Queen of witchdom and of night,
Work my will by magic rite.

In the earth and air and sea,
By the light of moon or sun,
As I pray, so mote it be.
Chant the spell, and be it done!
Queen of witchdom and of night,
Work my will by magic rite.

Doreen Valiente, 1957

Old Wives' Tales and Rhymes

A bit of fun to end the book. Many of these really make me smile, even if I am not convinced I believe them all!

At some time in our lives, all of us will have been guided in our actions by superstition or old wives' tales. Whether we have avoided walking under a ladder, or taken a lucky pen to use in an examination, whether we have thrown spilt salt over our shoulder or never worn a certain colour, it all comes down to the same thing; a belief, or a wish to believe, or even a fear of not believing, that our future can be influenced by events and things that probably have no obvious bearing upon it.

To believe in every superstition with which you have become acquainted would undoubtedly cause much confusion. What, for example, about the occurrence of ominous happenings in sequence? What if you were to see a black cat cross your path, and then see a solitary magpie? Does this mean that the bad luck of seeing a solitary magpie cancels out the good luck of having a black cat cross your path? Or is one occurrence a stronger influence on future events than the other and if so, which? Or are you destined to have a spell of good luck, swiftly followed by a spell of bad luck?

Superstitions can be personal, as in the case of the 'lucky' exam pen, or they can be common to whole communities, or even have influences worldwide. Superstitions may be as old as the hills, or they may be the result of a more contemporary folklore. Whatever the origins of some superstitions they are certainly fascinating to study.

Animals

bat: Many believe that a bat flying close to you is unlucky, especially if you hear it squeak as it approaches. Nevertheless, bats are not despised by all superstitions, for many people believe that is lucky to have bats nesting in your house. Nowadays, as bats become rarer, especially in urban settings, it should certainly be seen as a privilege.

cat: The cat is associated with a great many superstitions. Watch your cat carefully—cats are supposed to have a certain amount of extra-sensory perception. Strange behaviour in your cat may be its reaction to something that it has sensed that is beyond your perception. Does the cat appear nervous or frightened in your new house? There may be ghosts!

If your cat sneezes three times, count the sneezes. One sneeze is considered to be lucky, but three sneezes and you should prepare for an outbreak of colds and coughs in the family.

If a cat suddenly and unaccountably leaves home, some bad fortune will befall the family.

If you kill a cat, or even just tread on its tail, you will be very unlucky.

A black cat crossing your path will bring you good luck, but a white one is unlucky.

If a stray black cat should venture into your home, you should make it welcome, for this will bring you great good fortune.

Cats are also supposed to be able to forecast the weather. If your cat sits with its back to the fire, a storm is likely. If it spends too long washing itself, prepare for wet weather. If it seems to be inordinately frisky, the wind could soon become a gale.

dog: Dogs, like cats, are believed to have extra sensory perception and are supposed to have the ability to sense death and to see ghosts. Thus, a dog who howls without reason at the door is often seen as an omen of imminent death in the household.

Many people believe that dogs have a sense of 'good' and 'bad' people and that a person whom your dog takes a dislike to for no apparent reason may be an undesirable person to have as a friend. It is also widely believed that if you are followed home by a stray dog, this is a sign of good luck.

hare: A hare crossing your path is widely held to be an omen of ill-fortune, and a hare passing a house foretells a fire in the house in the future. At one time it was believed that witches chose to disguise themselves as hares.

hedgehog: Hedgehogs are generally thought to be lucky creatures. Passing a hedgehog on the road is a sign of good luck to come. Of course, killing a hedgehog is consequently unlucky.

horse: A white horse may be lucky; if you see one you should make a wish. If you meet a white horse whilst out with your beloved, it is said that you can be sure of happiness together in the future.

A piebald horse is also believed to be lucky, but only if you meet it head-on.

Finding a horseshoe is widely believed to bring good luck, but you must keep it after you find it if you want the luck to stay with you.

lamb: The lamb is the sign of peace and love in superstition as much as in religion. Meeting a lamb out on its own is a sign of good luck.

mouse: A gift of a white mouse will be lucky for you, but a grey mouse will not bring good fortune.

mule:
Mules are thought to be unlucky, and a sign of treachery.

rabbit: Rabbits have come to be regarded by some as symbols of fertility and fruitfulness; this idea most likely has its origins in the prolific breeding habits of the rabbit.

The belief that a rabbit's foot will bring luck and offer protection from harm is one that is held in many places throughout the world; to carry a rabbit's foot is lucky and, conversely, to lose one is most unfortunate.

On the first day of every month, many people consider that it is important to say "white rabbits" three times for luck.

toad: To find a toad sitting in one's path is thought to be a sign of money to come. Killing a toad is said to bring rain.

Apples

The apple is principally associated with superstitions concerning affairs of the heart, probably because of its associations with Adam and Eve. If a girl is able to peel an apple in one piece without breaking the peel, she should throw it over her left shoulder. If, on examining the peel after it has fallen, she is able to make out the shape of a letter, this is thought to be the first initial of the man whom she will marry. If the peel breaks into more than one piece when it falls to the floor, then the girl will not marry.

If you are uncertain as to whether your feelings of affection for another are likely to be returned, eat an apple and then throw a seed on the fire, saying as you do so, the name of the one you love. If the apple seed makes a popping sound as it burns, then you can rest easy that your love is not unrequited!

It is thought to be lucky if you do not pick up all the windfalls from your apple tree, but instead leave one or two where they lie on the ground.

Many people in Great Britain hold the belief that to see apple blossom and fruit on the same tree at the same time is a bad omen that means that there will be a death in the family.

Babies

There are countless superstitions concerning babies worldwide, probably stemming from the anxiety all new mothers feel about their babies and the responsibilities of bringing up a child.

Monday's child is fair of face;
Tuesday's child is full of grace;
Wednesday's child is full of woe;
Thursday's child has far to go;
Friday's child is loving and giving;
Saturday's child works hard for a living.
But the child that is born on the Sabbath day
Is bonny and blithe and good and gay.

It is said that a baby who is born with a cawl over his or her face will be lucky and grow to be rich.

A child who is born at twilight when the light is poor will grow up with second sight.

A baby who is born on Good Friday will grow used to sadness throughout its life but will, however, have the gift of easing other people through their own pain and distress.

A child who is born on All Hallow's Eve will be blessed with the gift of second sight.

A newly born baby is said to be in danger from the fairies until it first sneezes. From that moment on, it will be able to stay safely in the human world.

Rocking an empty cradle has two different superstitions attached to it— one is that a woman who rocks an empty cradle will have many babies, the other is that to rock an empty cradle means that the baby who usually sleeps in the cradle will die young.

If a baby's first tooth appears in its lower jaw, this is said to mean that the child will live long. If the baby grows teeth early, it is said that another child will be born in the family within a short time.

Many people believe that a baby should not see its own reflection in a mirror until six months after its birth, for a child who sees itself in a mirror before the age of six months will die before it is a year old.

It is believed to be better for a mother to nibble off the nails of her young baby with her teeth, because to cut a baby's nails before it is twelve months old is said to mean that the child will grow up to be light-fingered.

Dressing a baby in black is thought to be unlucky.

If a baby laughs or crows and kicks with its little hands open, it is said that the child will grow up open-handed and generous. A child who keeps its fingers firmly curled together, however, will grow up to be close-fisted, or mean.

Birds

It is considered unlucky for a bird to fly in to a house through an open window. A swallow entering a house through a chimney foretells a death in the household.

It is also considered to be unlucky to keep an injured wild bird in the house.

cockerel: If a cock crows with its head facing towards the house, there will be a visit from a stranger shortly.

If a girl is thinking of her sweetheart and hears the sound of a cockerel crowing, it is thought to be lucky, but if a man or woman hears a cockerel crowing on the day of their wedding, they may take this to mean that the marriage may not be a harmonious one.

An encounter with a white cockerel is thought to be unlucky.

crow: It is considered to be unlucky to see a crow standing on one leg, to have a crow flying and cawing round about your house, or to see two crows fighting outside your house.

If you hear the sound of a crow cawing, try the following to see what the future has in store—placing one foot right in front of the other, pace out the length of your shadow in footsteps. Add thirteen to this number, then divide the result by six. If the remainder is one, then you will be lucky, but two can only mean trouble and sorrow in store. Three means great happiness to come, four means you will never want for food and five means that you will be blessed with riches in later life.

cuckoo: to hear the first cuckoo of spring too early, in March, may bring you ill-fortune. If you hear it whilst lying in bed, you can expect to suffer from ill-health.

If you see a cuckoo and it is standing still, you are likely to remain settled where you are for some time, but to see a cuckoo take off into flight presages a move of some sort, or travel for the person who sees it.

For those who seek to know when they will marry, the sound of the cuckoo can help. On hearing the first cuckoo of the year, they should kiss their hand and wave it towards the sound of the cuckoo's call, saying as they do—"Cuckoo, tell me true, when shall I be married?"

When they hear the cuckoo again, they should count the number of its calls before it becomes silent once more. The number of calls will be the number of years that will pass before the wedding takes place.

To hear a cuckoo on the right hand side means that prosperity will come, but to hear it on the left is a sign of bad luck ahead.

dove: the dove is a sign of love and happiness and it is especially lucky for lovers who set eyes on it together.

duck: the sound of a quacking duck is thought by some to be lucky, as is the sight of a duck in flight.

eagle: the sound of the cry of an eagle in flight is thought to be a warning of doom.

geese: geese make very useful 'watchbirds', and possibly as a consequence of this, the sound of cackling geese is thought to be a warning of dangers unseen.

hen: if you hear a hen crowing like a cockerel instead of clucking as it should, bad luck, or more particularly, poor health may follow.

magpie: it is believed by some that to see a magpie flying from right to left across your path will bring you bad luck.
More generally, it is believed to be unlucky to see a solitary magpie. This idea perhaps has its origins in the fact that it is more common to see magpies in pairs. To see one on its own, therefore, suggests that somehow all is not right.

It is said by some people that one way of fending off the bad luck of seeing a single magpie is to look at the bird and speak to it, saying, "Good morning, Mr. Magpie." Alternatively, you could try spitting three times over your left shoulder.

If you see one magpie, always look around for others; there probably will be at least one other. Count them and remember the rhyme:

'One for sorrow,
Two is for joy.
Three for a girl,
Four is for a boy.
Five for silver,
Six is for gold.
Seven for a secret,
Never to be told.'

Another old rhyme says:

'One means anger,
Two brings mirth.
Three is a wedding,
Four is a birth.
Five is christening,
Six is a death.
Seven is heaven,
Eight is hell,
But nine is the very Devil's ain sel'.'

owl: owls are generally considered to be quite unlucky. It is thought to be unlucky to hear an owl hooting at night and to hear it hooting three times in succession bodes particularly ill as it may foretell that you will hear of someone's death.

peacock: peacock's feathers should not be brought into the house as this is considered to be very unlucky indeed. The 'eye' in a male peacock's tail feathers is thought to be evil.
It is considered to be lucky to see a peacock spreading out its feathers in courtship display.

raven: the raven, much like the crow, is generally considered to be a bird of ill-fortune. It is thought to be an omen of death to hear a raven crowing over your house.

The ravens that inhabit the Tower of London are famous worldwide, as is the superstition associated with them that if for some reason they all die, or fly away, or simply disappear, disaster will fall upon the country and its royal family.

robin: it is said that whoever hurts a robin or a wren will never prosper on land or at sea.

Bread

The idea of the baker's dozen, i.e. thirteen, is thought to come from an old belief that the baker had to keep his peace with the Devil and thus baked 'twelve for the baker and one for the Devil.'

If you are slicing bread and the slices are uneven, you may have been telling lies. If the bread crumbles as you slice it, beware of family quarrels.

Wasting bread is unlucky—if you throw it away today, you will go hungry later.

Candle

Candles should always be placed as securely as possible in their holders, for it is said to be unlucky if a candle falls over. This superstition may well have some foundation in the fact that an upset candle is a fire hazard and therefore can indeed bring very bad fortune.

In candle magick, flames must never be blown out. Extinguish with a snuffer or let them burn out on their own.

Christenings

There are many people who still believe that a baby will not thrive properly until it has been christened.

It is considered very lucky for a child to be christened on the same day of the week as that on which it was born.

A baby who cries at his or her own christening is fortunate. The cries are a sign that it is strong enough to fight the influence of evil. A baby that does not cry at its christening is not so lucky, however.

It is believed that the woman who carries the baby to church to be christened should carry a piece of bread and some cheese with her. This should be given to the first person whom she meets, on behalf of the child. If the food is not eaten or if the gift is refused, it is thought to be unlucky.

Good fortune will come to the baby if the gift is well-received, particularly if the recipient is poor or needy and eats the bread and cheese immediately.

Cigarettes

Many people, especially older people who remember relatives who fought in the war, believe that it is unlucky to light more than two cigarettes with one match. This is because those who fought in the wars thought that the first light gave snipers first sight of their target, and the second allowed them to take aim. Lighting a third person's cigarette would give a sniper time to shoot at the flaming target that the match provided.

Clothes

Dress carefully! Try not to put on any item of clothing inside out or to fasten any buttons wrongly; you will only be inviting misfortune, or so it is said. If you do put on any clothes inside out, you should keep them on that way for the rest of the day.

Always put some money in the right hand pocket of any coat or jacket that you wear for the first time, or any coat or jacket that you give to someone as a gift. This is said to protect the wearer against pennilessness in the future. A coat worn for the first time without money in the pocket may bring hard times upon the wearer.

If your shoelace comes undone accidentally, without being caught on anything and pulled out, you should be assured that your true love is thinking of you at that very moment.

Gloves are an unlucky gift to give unless the giver receives something in return.

Colour

green: Many people, particularly those in the acting professions, avoid wearing the colour green as it is thought to be unlucky. Some people believe that the wearer of a green dress will soon be wearing the black of mourning. Green is not thought to be unlucky, however, for those people who have birthdays in May.

brown: It is unlucky for anyone—bride, groom or guest—to wear brown to a wedding. Brown is a symbol of gradually fading affection.

It is said that someone who wears brown all year long will be working hard all year for the benefit of somebody else and not for his or her own good.

black: Although it is the colour of mourning, black is not considered to be an unlucky colour in itself, and is in fact considered to be a good colour for those who have December or August birthdays. It is also considered to be quite lucky to wear a hat that has a touch of black on it.

orange: Orange-red or flame colours worn at a wedding say that the partnership is based on selfishness and fortune-seeking rather than true love.

Ears

Many things are said about the size and shape of people's ears and the personalities that are associated with them.

Big ears are generally thought to indicate a generous nature, while small ears point to a certain meanness.

Ears that lie very close to the head are said to indicate timidness, even cowardliness, but sticking-out ears are the sign of a fighter.

Long or prominent ears indicate a musical person.

'My ears are burning, someone is talking about me.'

To feel a tingling sensation in the ears is an indication that someone is talking about you. If your right ear tingles, bad things are being said.

If the left ear tingles, someone is speaking favourably about you. As the saying goes—"The left for love and the right for spite."

Eyes

The shape, the colour, the position and the amount of white around the eye can all influence some people in their 'reading' of a person's character. For example, a person who has white showing under the pupils of his or her eyes is said to be of noble character and laudable lifestyle. Deep set eyes are thought by some to indicate shrewdness.

Brown eyes are supposed to be the kindest, whilst blue-grey eyes indicate generosity. The list of attributes is long and varies considerably. Perhaps it is fairest to say that people are judged to some extent by their appearance and features that appeal to some will not be attractive to others.

If your right eye itches, it is said that you are about to suffer a disappointment. If the left eye itches, things look more promising—you could be in for a pleasant surprise!

Styes are a painful and fairly common affliction of the eye. They will disappear of their own accord, but many people believe it to be helpful to rub the stye gently with a gold ring.

Eyebrows

'Trust not the man whose eyebrows meet,
For in his heart you'll find deceit.'

Feet

It is considered to be luckier to put your right foot out of bed first in the morning.

If your feet are itchy, you may be about to go on a journey.

If you wear your shoes out on the inside of the foot first, it is said that you are mean. If you wear them out on the outside of the foot first, you may be inclined to be extravagant.

Flirts, it is said, will wear out the toes of their shoes first.

Flowers

There are countless superstitions concerning flowers, their meanings and their properties. The following examples are a selection of some of these.
Many nurses take great pains to avoid combining red and white flowers in the same vase in their hospital wards—this combination is said to be very unlucky and signify death. It is also considered to be unlucky for hospital patients to take home their flowers when they are discharged. It is said to mean that they will soon be back in their hospital bed.
Picking up a flower that someone else has cut or picked and then dropped is said to be unlucky.

clover:

The belief that finding a four-leafed clover brings good luck to the finder is widespread. If the finder then passes the clover onto someone else, it is said that his or her good luck will increase.

daffodil:

It is unlucky to pick and take a single daffodil and take it inside. Always take a bunch.

daisy:

It is said that girls can find out the true feelings of their sweethearts by picking a daisy and plucking out the petals one by one, saying alternately with each petal plucked, "He loves me, he loves me not."

dandelion: Use a dandelion seed-head if you want to find out if the one

you love loves you. Blow away the seeds and with each puff say alternately, "he loves me, he loves me not."

If you want to find out how many years it will be until you marry the one you love, count the number of puffs it takes until all the seeds have gone.

gorse: The flowers of the gorse bush are unlucky to have in the house.

heather: White heather is considered by many people to be lucky, but it is better to grow it than to buy it.

lilac: White lilac flowers are considered to be unlucky and should not be taken into the house.

marigold: If you pick marigolds that you have grown yourself, it is said that you will become a drunkard.

may: Bringing may blossom into the house will bring bad luck, it is said.

orange blossom: Orange blossom is traditionally considered to be lucky to have at a wedding. It has associations with fertility.

pansies: Picking pansies when it is sunny is said to cause rain.

poppies: Never take poppies into the house because they are considered by some to be quite unlucky in this instance. It is also believed that staring into the centre of a poppy will cause temporary loss of vision.

snowdrops: Although a harbinger of spring and hence of new life, snowdrops are thought to be unlucky to have in the house, particularly if there is a sick person within.

Food and Drink

Making the tea weaker than usual may be an indication that a friend is turning away from you.

If the coffee pot rocks while it heats on the stove a visitor will be coming, it is said.

Don't worry if the soup continues to boil after you have taken it off the cooker—it is a sign that you will live to a ripe old age.

If the bread that you are baking burns, it is said to be a sign that someone is angry with you.

If a cork pops out of a bottle suddenly, beware, for you have a secret enemy.

The wine should always be passed round the table to the right, in a clockwise direction, following the course of the sun.

Do not fret if you drop a custard pie or any other pie in which eggs are ingredients. If it falls to the floor, you may be destined to be rich!

If you inadvertently cross two forks over one another, you may take it as a sign that you may be the subject of malicious gossip and slander in time to come.

If you drop a fork, you can expect a visit from a woman friend.

Stirring with a fork instead of a spoon is considered to be unlucky.

If you want the food that you are preparing to taste good, you should always stir it in a clockwise direction.

Some say that it is unlucky if two knives are crossed by chance, for it is seen as a bad sign, foretelling quarrelling, or worse.

If a knife falls to the floor and ends up with its blade sticking in the floor, it can be taken as a sign, it is said, that a visitor is on the way.

Spinning a knife on the table is also thought to be unlucky.

Hallowe'en

If a girl wishes to see who her future lover will be, she should try sitting alone in front of a mirror in candlelight on Hallowe'en, eating an apple. A vision of her true love should appear in the mirror, looking over her shoulder towards the glass. The girl should not turn round, but should go on eating the apple and looking into the mirror until the vision fades.

To answer any questions on Hallowe'en, run a new silk thread through a gold ring and hold it over a tumbler of water. Ask one question that can be answered with a direct 'yes' or 'no'. Hold the ends of the thread steadily as you ask, then notice how many times the ring strikes against the glass. If once, the answer is 'no'. If the ring strikes the glass twice, the answer is 'maybe', and if the ring strikes the glass three times, the answer is 'yes'. *See also* BABIES.

Hands

If the palm of your hand is itchy, it is said that you are going to be rich. It is also said that rubbing the itchy hand on wood is a way of assuring that the foretold wealth actually comes to you.

Insects

ants: It is quite commonly believed that to step on an ant will cause rain to come.

bees: Many people, especially in rural areas, believe that it is unlucky to kill a bee.
A swarm of bees that appears from nowhere and lands on your property is thought to be unlucky, foretelling death, but it is lucky to be given a hive of bees as a gift.

beetles: As with ants, it is believed that stepping on beetles will bring wet weather.

ladybirds: Ladybirds are generally considered to be lucky creatures and you are very fortunate if one of these delightful little insects lands upon you.

Ladder

The belief that it is unlucky to walk under a ladder is possibly one of the most widely known superstitions and is one that is believed by a great number of people, although most of them will not know why it is supposed to be so unlucky. The superstition possibly stems from the fact that when a ladder is raised up against a wall, it forms a triangle with the wall and the ground. The triangle is seen as representing the Holy Trinity and to walk through this is seen as an affront to God. As to what will happen to you if you do walk under a ladder, accounts vary. Some say that young girls who walk under ladders will never marry. Some take the act as an omen of death. Others see it as a portent of bad luck in general.

Laughing

"Laugh before breakfast tears before supper."

Mirror

The breaking of a mirror will bring seven years of bad luck down upon the person who breaks it.

It is believed that a child who sees its own reflection in a mirror before it is six months (some say a year) old will not live long. It is considered unlucky for a bride to look at her reflection in a mirror when she is dressed in her wedding clothes, before she is married.

Some people consider it to be unlucky to look at their reflection in a mirror after dark, or by candlelight.

Months

January: A mild January is supposed by some to be a forecast of a poor harvest.

Children who are born on New Year's day are considered to be lucky for the household into which they are born.

March: It is believed that a wet March will mean a poor harvest that year.

May: Some people believe that it is unlucky to get married in the month of May.

Moon

The Moon was associated in days past with an influence on the growth of hair and nails. From this stems the superstition that it is best to have your hair cut while the moon is waxing so that it grows strong and healthy. The same applies to the cutting of nails.

It is believed by some that it is wrong to point at the moon.

Some country folk still hold firm to the belief that it is best to sow seeds while the moon is on the increase.

It is considered by some to be unlucky for a child to be born when the moon is on the wane.

Some people used to believe that it was dangerous to sleep in the moonlight or to face the moon whilst sleeping, for it led to blindness, or being 'moonstruck', a mild form of madness.

'Washing' your hands in moonlight was thought by some to be a cure for warts.

It is thought to be unlucky to see a new moon for the first time through a window.

A wish made while looking up at a new moon is said to come true before the end of the year.

Nails

It is best to cut your nails while the moon is on the increase if you want them to grow strong. If you worry about which day to choose for cutting your nails, the following rhyme may help:

Cut your nails on Monday, cut them for news;
Cut them on Tuesday for a new pair of shoes;
Cut them on Wednesday, cut them for health;
Cut them on Thursday, cut them for wealth;
Cut them on Friday, a sweetheart to know;
Cut them on Saturday, a journey to go;
Cut them on Sunday, you cut them for evil,
For all the next week you'll be ruled by the Devil.

New Year

Just before midnight strikes on New Year's Eve, open a window in your house to let the Old Year out and the New Year in.

The first person to set foot in your house in the New Year should be a dark man. It is also believed that this man, the 'first foot', should not enter the house through the same door by which he came in; if he comes in the back door, he should leave by the front and vice versa.

It is thought to be unlucky to take something out of the house at New Year unless something has been brought in first. This should preferably be a lump of coal. Thus, the best thing to happen to a household at New Year is for a dark man to arrive after the stroke of midnight, carrying a lump of coal.

It is thought unlucky for your first visitor of the New Year to be fair-haired, or, worse still, a woman!

If your cupboards are not well stocked at New Year, it is said that you may go hungry in the coming twelve months.

It is thought to be advisable to wind up all the clocks in the house to ensure good luck, and to clean the house thoroughly on New Year's Eve.

Nose

A nose bleed is though by some to be a sign that the afflicted person is close to another for whom they feel a great deal of affection, perhaps someone with whom they are in love.

An itchy nose is said, according to different schools of thought, to be either a sign that you are angry, or that you will have a quarrel, or that you will be kissed by a fool, or that you will receive news or a letter.

Pins

"See a pin and pick it up,
All the day you will have good luck.
See a pin and let it lie,
Luck will surely pass you by."

If you spill a box of pins, try to ensure that you prevent some of them from falling out. If some pins are left in the box, you may get a pleasant surprise. If all the pins fall out of the box, you are likely to suffer a disappointment.

Plants

bracken: Bracken is though to be lucky to hang in the house. It is said to protect the building against the effects of thunder and lightning.
Destroying bracken is thought to cause wet weather.

chicory: The chicory plant is considered by some to bring good luck to travellers if they carry a root of the plant in their pocket.

ivy: Ivy is thought to be a lucky plant to have growing on the walls of your house. Ivy inside the house, on the other hand, is thought by some people to be unlucky, even if it is for the Christmas decorations!

mandrake: The mandrake plant has a strange-shaped root which is said by some to resemble the shape of a human. Folklore tells that when a mandrake root is pulled up, it emits a terrible shrieking sound. For this reason, many people avoided trying to dig up this plant. However, it was also thought to have curative properties and was used in various sorts of medicaments. In order for the screaming of the roots to be avoided, it was believed to be best to have the plant dug up by a dog.

mistletoe: Mistletoe is thought of as part of the traditional Yuletide decorations. It should not be hung in church because of its ancient associations with the Druids, to whom the plant was sacred.
Kissing under the mistletoe at Christmas time is said to guarantee lifelong friendship with those whom you kiss and it is considered to be unlucky to refuse to be kissed under the mistletoe.

myrtle: Myrtle is considered to be a plant symbolic of love. Myrtle that grows in your garden should be carefully tended, for to allow it to die is to invite ill-fortune.

rosemary: A branch of rosemary hung at the door, or rosemary growing near the door, is said protect the house from evil spirits and plague.

Sprigs of rosemary in the bridal bouquet should bring happiness at a wedding.

sage: Sage is said to be helpful in practices of divination. If a girl wishes to know who she will marry, she can go out at midnight on Hallowe'en and pluck nine sage leaves, as the clock strikes the hour. Then she should be able to see the face of her future husband.

Salt

Spilling salt is thought to be unlucky. If you do spill some inadvertently, take a pinch of it and throw it over your left shoulder. It is thought that this practice could stem from a belief that the thrown salt would blind the Devil, who sits on the left. On the other hand, the practice could originate from times when salt was a valuable commodity. The throwing of the salt over the left shoulder could then be seen as a bribe for the Devil, to dissuade him from doing you any harm.

There is a superstition that if you borrow salt, you should not pay it back for this would be unlucky. Some people hold that the borrowing or lending of salt in itself is unlucky.

Throwing salt onto the fire is a practice intended to ward off witches.

A dish of salt placed on or by the corpse of a dead person was thought to protect the dead person in some way.

Bathing a new baby in salt water, or placing a small bag or sachet of salt somewhere about the baby's clothing, was thought to have a protective effect.

Silver

Silver coins are generally thought to bring luck. The practice of keeping a lucky coin, particularly a silver one, is quite widespread.

The practice of crossing a gypsy's palm with silver was thought to act as a charm against evil, or at the very least, against the wrath of the gypsy!

Sneezing

Sneeze on Monday, sneeze for danger;
Sneeze on Tuesday, kiss a stranger;
Sneeze on Wednesday, get a letter;
Sneeze on Thursday, something better;
Sneeze on Friday, sneeze for sorrow;
Sneeze on Saturday, see your true love tomorrow;
Sneeze on Sunday, the Devil will have you for the rest of the week.

One a wish,
Two a kiss,
Three a letter,
Four is better,
Five a journey you will make,
Six an offer you should take.

It is thought that one sneeze is unlucky, but two are lucky.

The custom of saying "bless you" to someone who sneezes probably has its origins in the days of the plague, when sneezing was one of the first signs of the dreaded illness. As the plague almost inevitably ended in death, the blessing was more of an acknowledgement of the sneezing person's approaching demise.

Spider

'If you wish to live and thrive
Let the spider run alive.'

Killing a spider is widely thought to bring bad luck. Finding a little red money-spider on you can be taken as an indication of coming good fortune.

Thirteen

Thirteen is widely thought of as an unlucky number. Judas was the thirteenth man at the last supper and it was he who betrayed Jesus and brought about his death. Because of this, some believe it to be most unlucky to have thirteen people dining at the table together. Some believe that the setting of a fourteenth place will stave off misfortune.

Many hotels do not have a room number thirteen, and some streets do not have a house with that number.

I don't believe thirteen is unlucky, in numerology it has the vibration stability, security and maturity,

Trees and bushes

To catch an autumn leaf before it falls to the ground, before the end of October, is thought to be lucky.

aspen: the aspen is well known as the tree that still trembles with shame as it remembers its wood being used for the cross upon which Jesus was crucified. It was also believed to be a cure for aigue, or 'flu. The sufferer was supposed to cut a strand of hair and tie it to an aspen tree, saying, "Aspen tree, Aspen tree, shake and shiver instead of me".

blackberry: the blackberry or bramble bush can be bowed over into an arch under which people may pass if they wish to find a cure for rheumatism, warts and other ailments.

elder: sprigs from the elder tree should not be taken into the house for they are unlucky, it is said. It is believed that Judas hanged himself from an elder tree.

horse chestnut: the horse chestnut tree is believed to have certain curative properties and people sometimes carry conkers in their pockets to ease their rheumatism.

oak: It was once thought possible to transfer one's toothache to an oak tree by cutting a lock of hair and placing it in a hole in the tree, simultaneously entreating the tree to take the toothache.
It is thought to be very unlucky to chop down an oak tree.

rowan: The rowan tree has long been considered to be effective in warding off evil spirits. For this reason it is often to be found at the gates of graveyards, or growing by the door or gate of a house, particularly in rural areas.

Umbrella

It is thought to be unlucky to open an umbrella indoors.
Some say that to open an umbrella when the weather is fair is to invite rain.

If you drop an umbrella or a walking-stick, you should let someone else pick it up for you.

Wash Day

'They that wash on Monday, have the whole week to dry.
They that wash on Tuesday, are not so much awry.
They that wash on Wednesday, will get their clothes so clean.
They that wash on Thursday, are not so much to mean.
They that wash on Friday, wash for their need.
But they that wash on Saturdays are dirty folks indeed!'

Weddings

Weddings that take place in May are thought to be ill-fated.

It is said that whichever one of the bride and groom is the first to fall asleep on the night after the wedding, she or he will die first.

Wedding cake is customarily shared out among the guests on the wedding day to give them good luck.

Girls who received a slice of wedding cake and put it under their pillows might be lucky enough to see their own future husband appear to them as they slept.

A flight of birds seen flying overhead by the bride on the morning of her wedding is said to be a sign of a happy marriage, with children to come.

It is unlucky for the bridegroom to see his future bride in her wedding dress before the marriage ceremony. For him to see the bride before the wedding on the wedding day, whatever she is wearing, is also thought by a great many people to be unlucky.

When dressing for her big day, it is customary for the bride to take heed of the following rhyme:

Something old, something new,
Something borrowed and something blue,
And a silver sixpence in your shoe.
See that the church is full to the brim
Before the bride is allowed to come in.

When setting the date of their wedding, the couple might care to acknowledge the following rhyme:
Monday for health,
Tuesday for wealth;

Wednesday the best day of all;
Thursday for losses,
Friday for crosses;
Saturday, no luck at all!

Once married, you should keep your wedding ring safely on your finger, for it is considered to be unlucky to remove it.

Yuletide

Most superstitions attached to Yuletide and Christmas are happy ones.

If a man is lucky enough to kiss a girl under the mistletoe, he should remove one berry for every kiss he is allowed. Optimistic men should therefore hang mistletoe with a good supply of berries!

If a girl has not been kissed under the mistletoe over the Yuletide, she can expect to remain single, for at least a year and a day thereafter.

If you kiss someone under the mistletoe, you will remain on good terms with them always and never quarrel.

If you want to guarantee weeks and weeks of happiness in the year to come, eat mince pies in as many houses as you can over Yuletide. Each mince pie eaten will bring a week of happiness in the coming year.

In the days when it was customary to have a Yuletide log to burn at Christmas, it was thought to be lucky if a small piece of it was not burned and was saved for the following Christmas. Another superstition held that it was unlucky for the Yuletide log to be touched by a woman with a flat foot or a man with a squint!

On Christmas Eve, a girl who wishes to know who her future true love will be should put her shoes one across the other in the form of the letter 'T' as she goes to bed at night. She should then recite this rhyme:

"I hope tonight my true love to see—
So I put my shoes in the form of a 'T'."

Alternatively, the girl could try walking backwards to a pear tree, if there is one nearby, and then circle around it nine times. A vision of her true love may then appear to her.

Good luck will come to those who have a stir of the Christmas pudding. Make a wish as you stir, but do not tell anyone what you have wished for or your wish will not come true.

Whatever you believe in at Christmas, remember that Father Christmas will come !

Further Reading

Gardner, Gerald, *The Meaning of Witchcraft*, 1959

Murray, Margaret, *The Witch-Cult in Western Europe*, 1921

Adler, Margot, *Drawing Down the Moon: Witches, Druids, Goddess-Worshippers, and Other Pagans in America Today*, Viking, 1979.

Farrar, Janet and Stewart, Bone, Gavin. *The Pagan Path*. Phoenix Publishing, 1995

Farrar, Janet and Stewart, *A Witches' Bible*, Robert Hale, 1997

Dunwich, Gerina, *The Wicca Book of Days*, Citadel Press, 1995.

Valiente, Doreen, *The Rebirth of Witchcraft*, Robert Hale, 2007

Valiente, Doreen, *Natural Magic*, Robert Hale, 1999

Valiente, Doreen, *An ABC of Witchcraft Past and Present*, Robert Hale, 1994

Valiente, Doreen, *Witchcraft for Tomorrow*, Robert Hale, 1994

Ravenwolf, Silver, To Ride a Silver Broomstick, Llewellyn Publications, 1994.

Cunningham, Scott, *Wicca: A Guide for the Solitary Practitioner*, Llewellyn Publications, 1988

The Stonewylde Series by Kit Berry, will published by Gollancz 2011: *Magus of Stonewylde*; *Moondance of Stonewylde*; *Solstice at Stonewylde*. *Shadows at Stonewylde*, will be out in hardback only on August 2011.

Links

Kit Berry:
www.stonewylde.com

Pagan Federation:
http://paganfed.org/

Janet Farrar and Gavin Bone:
http://www.callaighe.com/

http://doreenvaliente.org/
http://www.caw.org/
http://www.stregheria.com/
http://www.sacred-texts.com/
http://centre-for-pagan-studies.com/
http://www.geraldgardner.com/